Anatomy
of the
Ship

The
Type XXI U-Boat

Anatomy
of the
Ship

The
Type XXI U-Boat

Fritz Köhl & Eberhard Rössler

Naval
Institute
Press

1. Frontispiece

Slip 5 of the Deschimag AG Weser yard at
Bremen at the end of the war. From left to
right, the Type XXI boats are U3052,
U3042, U3048 and U3056, with the stern
sections of U3053, U3043 and U3079 in the
foreground and part of U3061 visible on slip
4 at the right.

First English language edition published in
Great Britain 1991 by
Conway Maritime Press Ltd,
24 Bride Lane, Fleet Street,
London EC4Y 8DR

© Conway Maritime Press Ltd 1991

Published and distributed in the United States
of America and Canada by the
Naval Institute Press, Annapolis,
Maryland 21402

First published in 1988 under the title
Ubootyp XXI
© Bernard & Graefe Verlag, Koblenz, 1988

Library of Congress Catalog Card No. 90-64374

ISBN 1-55750-829-1

Manufactured in Great Britain

Contents

PUBLISHER'S NOTE

Unlike most other titles in the Anatomy series, *Type XXI* was not written specially but was translated and adapted from an existing German publication. This has inevitably resulted in certain departures from the established format, notably in the inclusion of separate illustrated sections of text covering the construction process, Allied efforts to disrupt the building process by air attack, and details of the sophisticated but troublesome sonar fit of the Type XXI. In addition to these, we have been able to provide a specially-written general introduction to the Type XXI by Jak P Mallmann Showell.

The drawings also differ slightly from the established Anatomy style, being reproduced from Fritz Köhl's highly accurate interpretations of the original construction drawings.

Introduction

THE ELECTRO-SUBMARINE
by Jak P Mallmann Showell

The quest for a true underwater submarine capable of sustaining high speeds for long periods, which blossomed during the first decade of this century, was brought to a halt by the outbreak of World War I. Both Germany and Britain then chose to concentrate on diesel engines for surface and electricity for submerged propulsion. Although still in its infancy, the diesel principle showed great development potential and the heavy fuel oil had the advantage of not igniting easily in combat, making it much safer than volatile petrol. The majority of power sources of the day required air to work, and therefore electricity supplied from batteries was the only feasible way of propelling boats once they had left the surface.

Few designers pursued alternative propulsion systems after the war, although some interesting variations on the main theme were devised. The British, for example, built the large, steam propelled K Class, and there was talk of reviving pre-war ideas such as generating heat in a boiler powered by highly corrosive caustic soda. One of the most original ideas came from an engineer at the Krupp Germania Works in Kiel, Hellmuth Walter, who devised a closed-circuit propulsion system fuelled by hydrogen peroxide, which was capable of running underwater without air. Walter approached the Supreme Naval Command at a time when the Treaty of Versailles prevented Germany building or owning submarines. This did not mean, however, that Germany had lost interest in underwater warfare; simply that there was no possibility of financing large scale research.

Today it is well known that Germany kept abreast of submarine technology by maintaining a development bureau in Holland for the purpose of building submarines for foreign countries. Despite a healthy contribution from the German tax-payer, the resources of this bureau were limited to working with new patents and updating existing machinery. It could not attempt a great re-think of submarine technology, nor was it concerned with the evaluation of strategy. This point is as important as it is strange, because it was in marked contrast to Germany's general naval policy. The harsh restrictions of the Treaty of Versailles inspired naval planners to seek major improvements in ship technology, in order to gain maximum effect from the limited number of ships Germany was allowed. The results of this policy were monumental; among other things, a completely new concept, the pocket battleship, was created. Nevertheless, very little of this progress penetrated into the submarine sphere.

March 1935, when Hitler repudiated the Treaty of Versailles, was an important milestone in the creation of the Third Reich's armed forces, but the rapid remilitarisation which followed also had a detrimental effect on the development of the submarine. Rather than grasping the opportunity of using recently acquired technology to build a modern submarine fleet comparable with the advances made in other industrial fields, Germany chose the alternative policy of producing the largest possible number of boats in the shortest time. To achieve this, proven World War I designs were hurriedly modified, and the consequence was that the Submarine Arm began World War II with roughly the same technological combination as that with which it had ended the first War. Submarine speeds were slighly faster, engines could run for long periods with less noise, radio and sound detection techniques were better, but a World War I submariner would easily have been at home in the new boats which went to war in September 1939 and continued to form the backbone of the fighting at sea until the bitter end in 1945.

The consolidation of dictatorship in Germany also produced a misleading picture of German industrial and military might. Rather than the planned, monolithic industries envisaged in National Socialist ideology, German industry rapidly developed such diversification and duplication that the industrial base of Hitler's Reich was severely flawed from the beginning. This process also applied to many areas within the armed forces, and in the context of this book it can best be illustrated by the U-boat Arm: the men who determined policies and designs, as well as allocating monies, were at the Supreme Naval Command's U-boat Office in Berlin; the operational boats were commanded by Flag Officers based in the sea ports; boats belonging to the submarine school were controlled by the Torpedo Inspectorate; and construction took place in private yards. There was hardly any liaison between any of them!

The uncoordinated planning of the 1930s continued during the war to such an extent that aims formulated in late September 1939 for producing about thirty submarines per month were barely realised. In fact, construction increased at such an unsatisfactory pace that after a year of war Hitler had still not enforced decisions about future construction plans. Grand Admiral Erich Raeder (Supreme Commander-in-Chief of the Navy) was forced to intervene to prevent an actual decline in production levels. After a further year, Raeder tried again to press the issue of equal priority to the air force for the Submarine Arm, but the Russian campaign was consuming such vast resources that Hitler felt obliged to give higher priority to the Luftwaffe. Meanwhile, shortages of materials and equipment were made worse by the call up of skilled workers in the submarine building yards for national service.

U-BOATS AT WAR

The U-boat war came to a climax during the autumn of 1940, when a small number of U-boats, never more than a dozen at a time, reaped havoc in the shipping lanes of the Western Approaches. There were too few boats for true 'wolf pack' attacks, but occasionally a number converged on the same convoy for a devastating group attack. At this time an average of over five ships were sunk for every U-boat at sea. This so-called 'Happy Time' for the U-boats did not last long, however; the U-boat offensive started to collapse during the following spring, when the three aces Günter Prien (U47), Otto Kretschmer (U99) and Joachim Schepke (U100) were sunk. The diaries of the U-boat Command show 1941 to have been a hard struggle. 1942 saw a brief respite of a few months in which Germany reaped a rich harvest in United States waters, where initially there was little or no opposition. Although this period is often described as the 'Second Happy Time' or 'Second Golden Time', individual sinkings had dropped to an average of only two ships sunk for every U-boat at sea.

In the summer of 1942, when the American waters became untenable, Germany had virtually no alternative than return to the mid-Atlantic gap in Allied air cover, where considerable changes had taken place. The Royal Navy had utilised the lull during the U-boat offensive in United States waters to build up escort numbers and develop improved antisubmarine techniques, with the result that the German return to mid-Atlantic saw terrific opposition. Escorts made it difficult to approach targets and U-boats were pursued with a new vigour for much longer periods. In addition to this, the Bay of Biscay had also become noticeably more difficult for U-boats. Attacks there by the RAF were both frequent and determined, threatening the possible closure of the German Atlantic bases in France. The U-boat Arm urgently needed boats capable of crossing this dangerous area underwater.

In addition to a longer underwater range, the new boats had to be faster to evade convoy escorts. This latter point was made exceptionally clear by even the experienced commanders' inability to get into favourable attacking positions. In 1940, when the first U-boat aces were gaining their Knights Crosses, it was frequently possible for a boat to attack the same convoy several times, pausing just long enough to re-load torpedoes. By the autumn of 1942, this pattern had changed. U-boat commanders were lucky if they got close enough to shoot at a single ship. The majority never got closer to attacking than seeing the enemy on the horizon. In fact, it has been calculated that of the 1171 U-boats commissioned during the war, only about 321 actually inflicted damage on enemy shipping.

The biggest convoy battle of the war, when some forty ships of the fast convoy HX229 caught up with fifty-four ships of the slow convoy SC122, was fought in March 1943. Although this has been described as the climax in the Atlantic, many historians have overlooked the fact that this fateful March was the seventh month in which Germany had had over a hundred U-boats in the Atlantic. The daily average number of U-boats at sea rose from often less than ten in 1940 to fifty in January 1942 and seventy in July. Numbers then increased rapidly to one hundred in September, where the level remained until after March 1943. With so many at sea, it is no wonder that a clash of previously unknown proportions took place. The remarkable points are that Germany had over a hundred U-boats at sea for over half a year before this battle occurred, and that the average sinkings had dropped to only one merchant ship lost for every two U-boats at sea. This negative trend had been appreciated by the U-boat Command since before the

withdrawal from United States waters, and in November 1942 the U-boat Chief, Admiral Karl Dönitz, called a conference at his Paris headquarters to discuss means of regaining the initiative in the U-boat war.

THE BIRTH OF THE ELECTRO-SUBMARINE

The November 1942 meeting, attended by U-boat Command officers, engineers from the building yards and experts from the Naval Construction Office in Berlin, represented a significant point in the history of the submarine. The first point on the agenda was an update from Professor Hellmuth Walter on the progress of his project. In 1939 Dönitz had been instrumental in persuading the authorities to allow Walter facilities for building an experimental submarine. Although reduced in size to 80 tons, this craft (V80), had produced sensational results. In addition to good handling characteristics, it reached speeds of just over 26 knots, which was a vast improvement on the conventional submarine's best of about 8 knots. The Walter prototype was demonstrated to the Supreme Commander-in-Chief of the Navy, Grand Admiral Erich Reader, in February 1942, but neither he nor the Naval Construction Bureau had shown a great deal of interest. Even after Dönitz's intervention, the Naval Construction Office remained adamant in its view that concentration on the conventional Types VII and IX was preferable to the diversion of resources to experimental projects. The development of new types could clearly only take place at the expense of cutting back production of operational boats. In a way, Dönitz was being beaten with his own whip. Since the beginning of the war he had been asking for a large number of Type VIIC boats and now, when the High Command had abandoned its own plans in favour of stepping up production according to Dönitz's wishes, he apparently changed his mind to want something completely different.

The Naval High Command had good reasons for their stand against the new project. Walter's work was not without problems, and in November 1942 there was still an enormous gap between the small, fast experimental boat and a full scale operational version, capable of carrying fifty men into battle. One of the biggest problems was the volatile and highly concentrated hydrogen peroxide fuel, which could not be carried in conventional bunkers. Special rubber lined tanks were designed. On top of this, Walter's engine consumed the valuable liquid at such a high rate that the vast volumes posed a definite storage problem. The fuel tank would have to be as large as, or even larger than, the submarine itself! To overcome this, Walter had designed a double hulled boat, with one section below the other so as to form a figure 8 in section. The crew and machinery would occupy the upper part, while the lower hull would be one huge fuel tank. However, despite Walter's careful planning, there was little hope of having such a boat ready for the front in the rear future. Further experiments, using different machinery and larger boats, would be necessary before an ocean-going operational craft could be designed.

That November meeting would have ended on a disappointing note for the U-boat Arm had it not been for two submarine eningeers named Schürer and Bröcking. Listening to Walter's lecture, they came up with a simpler solution to Dönitz's problem. If the Admiral wanted higher under-water speeds and longer ranges, then why not just add another hull full of batteries underneath an ordinary submarine? The additional electrical capacity should provide the necessary power to meet requirements. A quick calculation showed the suggestions was indeed feasible. Thus at a stroke pre-World War I technology was adapted to the concept of the electro-

TABLE 1: **DESIGN PARTICULARS**

Type design	H Oelfken/OKM (June 1943)
Production design	Deschimag AG Weser, Bremen; Engineering Office Glückauf (IBG), Blankenburg (July-December 1943)
Basic construction	Vessel assembled from eight pre-fabricated sections. Planned overall building time approx 6 months, including only 50 days on the stocks.

TABLE 2: **WEIGHTS AS DESIGNED**

Hull construction	S1	Pressure hull	241.4t		
		Foundations, decks and internal tanks	75.4t		
		Outer hull	219.5t		
		Conning tower	10.6t		
		Other	27.0t		
			573.9t	573.9t	
	S2/3	Equipment		56.6t	
	S4	Paint and cement		6.0t	
		Building reserve S		10.0t	
				646.5t	646.5t
Machinery	M1	Diesel engine installation	64.8t		
		Shaft, transmission and propellers	37.4t		
		Electrical installation	40.9t		
		Battery system	238.8t		
		Other	1.0t		
			382.0t	382.0t	
	M2/3	Auxiliary systems		78.7t	
		Water, oil and air for M1/2		12.1t	
		Building reserve M		10.0t	
				482.8t	482.8t
Armament					75.1t
Fuel oil					231.1t
Engine oil					9.4t
Other stores					53.2t
Commission reserve					5.0t
Effective ballast (ballast weight minus ballast displacement)					107.1t
TOTAL:					1610.2t

submarine, which later became U-boat Type XXI. In retrospect it appears strange that no one had thought of this earlier.

THE ELECTRO PRINCIPLE

The term 'Electro-Submarine' may need a little explanation. Although it contained a similar propulsion system to that used in existing, conventional boats, the new design functioned on a different principle. All submarines of the day were primarily diesel-propelled surface craft, which dived only for comparatively short periods to evade the enemy or to launch rare submerged attacks. The reason for this was that their submerged cruising speeds were slower than a brisk walking pace on land, and even at their fastest they could be out-performed by a pedal cyclist. The electro-submarine was designed as a pure underwater craft, which would spend the majority of its time below the waves, running on electrical power from its huge batteries. It would cruise at schnorkel depth for re-charging the batteries with diesel engines, but, in contrast to existing submersibles, the new boat would not use its diesels as the primary propulsion source.

Already before the war the Royal Dutch Navy had used schnorkels fitted to conventional boats, but this idea had been suggested by Kptlt J J Wichers as a means of running diesel engines under the water to escape from oppressive tropical heat. The Dutch schnorkel was not designed to plunge submarines into a permanent underwater environment. After the war, the Type XXI principle was adopted by other countries and initially served as an intermediate stage between conventional submersibles and true submarines running with atomic reactors. Though atomic submarines were far superior in performance and were able to remain submerged for weeks and months on end, the electro principle has been adopted by navies all around the world under the modern name of Patrol Submarine.

CONSTRUCTION

Detailed theoretical calculations for the electro-sumbarine concept were completed by early January 1943, at about the same time as Dönitz succeeded Raeder as Supreme Commander-in-Chief of the Navy. The underwater performance was more than impressive. An electro-submarine was thought capable of maintaining fast speeds of 18 knots for 90 minutes or 12 knots for ten hours, or it could cruise silently at about 5 knots for 60 hours. This was indeed a fantastic improvement when one considers that the conventional Type VIIC, which bore the brunt of the fighting in the Atlantic, had a top submerged speed of about 6 knots for 45 minutes, or could cruise underwater at 2 knots for 20–30 hours. It is easy to see that the VIIC became virtually stationary once it left the surface and that the new boat could not only cross the dangerous Bay of Biscay, but also travel submerged into the convoy routes of the North Atlantic. The schnorkel would only have to be extended every other day for re-charging the batteries by diesel

engines. These performance figures still could not match the superior 26 knots plus of the closed-circuit Walter engine, but the older technology would make it easier and quicker to get production under way.

Initial planning and working drawings were complete by July 1943, when the forecast was made that the first electro boats of Type XXI would be ready by the end of 1944. The go-ahead to start production was given on Friday 13 August 1943, but the authorities stipulated that building and delivery schedules for the already obsolete Type VIIC/42 should not be curtailed. Hitler agreed only to a cut-back in the programme for the larger Type IX boats. By this time he had reversed his opinion of the air force and U-boats; the defeat of the Luftwaffe in the Battle of Britain had convinced him that the Atlantic was his most important front line, and that nothing should interrupt the flow of U-boats.

Progress with the electro-submarine was not easy. The new development was taking place at a time when war had already imposed drastic shortages on the shipbuilding industry. Much of the waterside construction space was being used to capacity and, on top of this, the shortages problem had a knock-on effect on other, inland industries where auxiliary equipment was being produced. Building the electro-submarine was not just a case of adding another hull with more batteries to an existing submarine design. Much of the interior equipment of the boats in service was also out-of-date. For example, since the finding of convoys and the penetration of their defensive ring had become the most difficult part of the attack, it was important to have more torpedoes ready for action: the ultimate was for all torpedoes to be carried in tubes from which they could be fired without the necessity for loading. The new XXI design was to start with six bow tubes and a semi-automatic hydraulic loading system, capable of filling all the tubes in about twenty minutes. This was considerably shorter than the time needed to re-load one tube manually in a conventional boat. It is worth noting also that both Types VII and IX had torpedo storage containers built into the space between the upper deck and the top of the pressure hull, but the contents could not be discharged until they had been manhandled into the boat and loaded into the firing tubes.

Depth-keeping had become another major headache because from mid-1942 onwards U-boats were frequently pursued with noisy vigour for long hours to make concentration difficult. To overcome this, the Type XXI was fitted with water pressure controlled depth keeping equipment. Crew comforts were improved by providing deep freezers to keep food in better condition. In addition to modifying existing equipment, the Type XXI also had to accommodate a whole range of innovations in equipment, such as radar, receivers for detecting the presence of enemy radar, sonar and new improved underwater listening gear.

Depsite the considerable progress made with the planning of the Type XXI, Dönitz was not happy with the forecast production schedules and approached the Armaments Minister, Albert Speer, to see whether these could be improved. Speer's Ministry had undertaken similar projects for other industrial processes, and it did not take long to design a mass production line. The basic concept was for a number of separate firms to build individual sections of the boat, and for these to be delivered to riverside yards for final assembly. It turned out that each basic unit would be too heavy for land-based transport, so only factories with river or canal access could be considered. In the end, it was decided to split the boat into eight sections, to be produced in thirteen different sites. Duplication of the construction process was important since enemy action could easily interfere with the process, or even put one or more factories out of production. Plans to put the entire assembly process under concrete went ahead as well, but this complex undertaking was expected to take longer than the manufacture of the first boats, and mass production started without bomb protection. A huge bunker, named Valentin, which had been under construction at Farge near Bremen since the beginning of 1943, turned out to be ideal for accommodating the Type XXI production line. However, the war ended before it was completed and the assembly of electro-submarines was carried out in the open at three yards: Blohm und Voss in Hamburg, Deschimag AG Weser in Bremen and Schichau in Danzig.

Obviously, with so many widely distributed contributors, a detailed timetable became of paramount importance and this was the weak point at which the Allies were able to attack the system. The scale of the undertaking made it impossible to conceal from the cameras of Royal Air Force Photo Reconnaissance Units, and well trained photo interpreters quickly noticed something was afoot. Even newsapers in neutral countries noted the evident preparations for a new German U-boat offensive. It was therefore not long before Allied bombers began to pay special attention to the shipyards. Nevertheless, despite an intensive bombing campaign which resulted in some production delays, comparatively little damage was done to the assembly lines and most continued in business until the end of the war. There were some delays and set-backs, however, as well as teething problems, and it perhaps no wonder that the schedule planned in 1943 was not met. It is, however, astonishing that the Type XXI project got as far as it did under war conditions.

Assessing the exact damage of the Allied bombing campaign is a little difficult because there are photographs of the slipways showing boats with considerable damage and captions noting that this had been caused by Allied bombs. There are, however, also pictures of the same boats without damage being inspected by British soldiers, which would suggest that the boats were destroyed by the British Army after the ceasefire, rather than by the Royal Air Force before it.

TABLE 3: BOATS DELIVERED AND COMMISSIONED

Dockyard	U-boats delivered	No of U-boats commissioned
Blohm & Voss, Hamburg	U2501–2546, 2548, 2551, 2552	48
Deschimag AG Weser, Bremen	U3001–3041, 3044–3046	41
Schichau, Danzig	U3501–3530	30
		TOTAL: 119

TYPE XXI OPERATIONS AT THE CLOSE OF THE WAR

The first Type XXI was launched as U2501, under the command of Oblt Otto Hübschen, at Blohm und Voss on 12 May 1944, much earlier than the schedule originally devised by the Naval Construction Office, so the Armaments Ministry had made a significant contribution to the speeding up of the building process. This boat, together with the next half dozen, suffered from defects which prevented it from being used for operational purposes. Furthermore, some vital electronic equipment was still unavailable, and the boats went on their first trials without it. This was, however, a minor inconvenience beside the achievement of instituting a large-scale and complex mass production process without first building even a prototype. The faulty craft were not wasted because they served for essential training and experimental purposes. It should be noted, however, that U2501 was not the first electro-submarine to be launched, since it had been decided during the initial development stages also to build a small coastal version of the design (denoted Type XXIII), of about 250 tons, the first of which went into the water at Deutsche Werft in Hamburg on 30 April 1944.

The first operational Type XXI, U2511, under the command of the ace Korvkpt Adalbert Schnee, sailed from Kiel to Norway on 18 March 1945, less than two months before the end of the war. Minor faults and some damage sustained during deep diving tests kept the boat in the repair yard at Bergen until the end of April, by which time half a dozen or so other Type XXI boats were ready to sail. U2511 was at sea when the order to stop hostilities came, but this did not prevent Schnee from launching a mock attack against a heavily defended British cruiser. Breaking through the escort screen, he continued until the target filled his periscope's field of vision, then aborted the attack and ordered the boat into the depths. This successful mock attack proved that the Type XXI lived up to expectations. Had it appeared a few years earlier, the fierce battles in the Atlantic might have had a different outcome.

At the end of the war, the following Type XXI boats had left Germany and were waiting in Norwegian ports:

Bergen	U2506 (Kptlt Horst von Schroeter)
	U3514 (Oblt Günther Fritze)
Stavanger	U3035 (Oblt Ernst-August Gerke)
Kristiansand	U2529 (Kptlt Fritz Kalipke)
Horten	U2502 (Kptlt Heinz Franke)
	U2513 (Korvkpt Erich Topp)
	U2518 (Kptlt Friedrich Weidner)

U3017 (Oblt Rudolf Lindschau)
U3041 (Kptlt Hans Hornkohl)
U3515 (Oblt Fedor Kuscher)

AFTER THE WAR

The following boats survived for more than a few months after the war:

U2513	Went to the United States and was scrapped in about 1956.
U2518	Handed over to France and served as *Roland Millirot*.
U2529	British N27 until 1947, then handed over to Russia.
U2540	Scuttled near the Flensburg lightship on 4 May 1945; raised in 1957 and recommissioned in the Federal German Navy as *Wilhelm Bauer*. Now being restored in the Maritime Museum at Bremerhaven.
U3008	Moved from Kiel to Britain and then on to the United States and used for experiments until about 1955.
U3017	Served as British N41 until scrapped in 1950.
U3035	British N28 until 1948, then handed over to the USSR.
U3041	British N29 until 1948, then handed over to the USSR.
U3515	British N30 until 1948, then handed over to the USSR.

The rest of the Type XXI boats were either sunk, scuttled in deep water or scrapped after the war.

I was most surprised early in 1985 when Gus Britton (Assistant Curator of the Royal Navy Submarine Museum at HMS *Dolphin*) asked me to identify a U-boat inside the old fitting-out bunker Elbe II in Hamburg. The puzzling point was that the boat had been visited by a British serviceman long after the war, at a time when all U-boats not in Allied navies were supposed to have been scrapped or sunk. I knew the area very well; in fact I had been there only a few months earlier and could clearly visualise huge piles of rubble preventing anything getting in or out of the ruin. This presented such a hazard to shipping that a massive wall had been built to prevent ships scraping the jagged concrete. Although highly incredible, it appeared possible that the boat might still be there. So I made arrangements for Wolfgang Hirschfeld (U-boat radio operator and naval historian) and myself to visit the bunker at low tide during the summer of 1985. It was a sensational experience to stand inside the ruins of an old bunker as the tide went down watching not one but three Type XXI boats appear to surface. Holes in the bunker allowed shafts of bright sunlight to illuminate the dim interior under the massive roof, which had fallen at an angle over the three boats. The bunker was so well built that it had defied Allied bombs and the postwar efforts of three salvage firms, all of which went bankrupt in the process of trying to remove it. Unfortunately, the demolition attepts resulted in the mutilation of the U-boats for scrap metal: two have lost conning towers and engine sections. The third, however, could not be touched because the several metres thick concrete roof is resting partly on top of it.

Within days of the ceasefire, a Royal Navy survey identified the boats scuttled inside the bunker as U3506, U3004 and U2505. Another U-boat, U2501, shown in a photograph in this book to be lying in front of the West Basin, was removed shortly after the war. Gerd Thäter, the last commander of U3506, and his Obermaschinist (Chief Mechanic) identified the easternmost boat, that lying trapped under the roof and shown in a photograph in this book, as their former boat.

TABLE 4: SECTION WEIGHTS AND VOLUMES

Section	Weight		Compartments	Volume
I	S	55t	Stern compartment	33cu m gross
	M	18t		23cu m net
	Other³	6t		
	TOTAL	79t		
II	S	68t	Engine room	124cu m gross
	M	52t		90cu m net
	Other³	10t		
	TOTAL	130t		
III	S	70t	Diesel engine room	171cu m gross
	M¹	71t		107cu m net
	Ballast	20t		
	Other³	8t		
	TOTAL	169t		
IV	S	56t	After accommodation	65cu m gross
	M²	12t		63cu m net
	Ballast	12t	Battery compartments 1.1 and 2.1	97cu m gross
	Other³	7t		63cu m net
	TOTAL	87t		
V	S	104t	Central control room	73cu m gross
	M	29t		58cu m net
	Conning tower	12t	Auxiliary machinery, magazines and refrigeration room	65cu m gross
				49cu m net
	Other³	10t	Conning tower	14cu m gross
	TOTAL	155t		10cu m net
VI	S	122t	Forward accommodation	133cu m gross
	M²	13t		129cu m net
	Ballast	29t	Battery compartments 1.2, 1.3, 2.2 and 2.3	201cu m gross
	Other³	8t		138cu m net
	TOTAL	172t		
VII	S	62t	Bow torpedo room	185cu m gross
	M	1t		168cu m net
	Ballast	26t		
	Other³	7t		
	TOTAL	96t		
VIII	S	57t		
	M	2t		
	Torpedo tubes	26t		
	Ballast	38t		
	Other³	7t		
	TOTAL	130t		

Notes
1 including diesel engines   2 excluding batteries   3 including lifting machinery   4 including tube doors
S = Structure   M = Machinery

So, apart from *Wilhelm Bauer*, three Type XXI boats have survived the war to lie on the surface at low tide. It must be emphasised that access is most difficult and dangerous, and their resting place is in a restricted area surrounded by private land. Casual visits are not possible, but perhaps one day the true significance of these three wrecks will be appreciated. The accomplishment of this breakthrough in submarine design in such a comparatively short period of time, under the constant pressures of war, represents one of the great technological achievements of our times. Those three wrecks, as well as the museum boat *Wilhelm Bauer*, are great technical monuments.

Construction

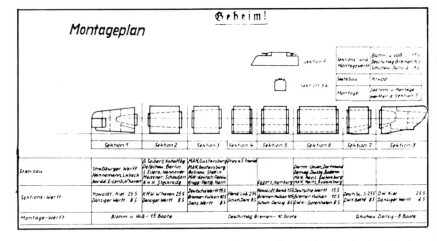

Figure 1. The original production plan for the Type XXI, carefully planned with the assistance of the Armaments Ministry.

The assembly of the Type XXI boats from prefabricated sections was one of the most innovative features of the class. The illustrations in this section give an impression of the construction process, and the text details the Allied attempts to destroy by air attack the most important assembly yard, Blohm & Voss in Hamburg. Further photographs illustrate the extent of bomb damage at Blohm & Voss and at the other major assembly yard, Deschimag AG Weser in Bremen.

2. Seven sections for Type XXI boats, destined never to be assembled, on a parking area at the Veersmann Quay in the port of Hamburg. At the front and in the centre are three No 6 sections, containing the forward living quarters and four battery compartments. These were the largest sections of the Type XXI, and were built by the Deutsche Werft at Finkenwärder; they were destined for the Blohm & Voss assembly dockyard. On the left and in the background are three No 3 sections. They contain the diesel engine rooms, and were also built by Finkenwärder. A central section, No 5, is parked on the right-hand side. The upper deck and conning tower are still missing, but the stubs of the hatches to the central control room and the galley are clearly visible, as are the two periscopes and various other pieces of extending apparatus.

3. Lowering the bow section 8 onto a special transport raft in the dock basin at the Danzig Dockyard. The other sections built by the Danzig yard for the Type XXI U-boat – sections 2, 3 and 1 – are already lashed down on the raft. This raft then transported the sections to the Schichau assembly dockyard.

4. The installation of the starboard MAN M6V 40/46 diesel engine in Section 3 of a Type XXI U-boat at AG Weser. The exhaust flaps located above the engine are already fitted, but the diesel gearboxes are absent.

5. U2501 on 12 May 1944, shortly before her launch, in slip 6 of the Blohm & Voss yard at Hamburg. She was the first Type XXI U-boat to be commissioned, on 27 June 1944; the Allied invasion of Normandy was well under way, and Allied forces were entering Cherbourg, the first major port. U2501 was forced to return to the dockyard for ten days in early July due to damage, and subsequently began her UAK and training period in the Baltic. The first Commander of this boat was Oblt Otto Hübschen. The decision had been made while the vessel was still under construction that U2501 was not to see service at the front. She remained at Hamburg after her return there, serving from November 1944 as the KLA training boat.

AIR ATTACKS ON THE ASSEMBLY YARDS

At quite an early stage the British acquired details of many of the characteristics of the Type XXI U-boat, and of the German plans for putting the new machine into service. They obtained information partly through the interrogation of prisoners, but principally as a result of outstanding aerial reconnaissance, coupled with excellent photograph interpretations. In early May 1944 a Naval Intelligence Office report stated that Germany had practically stopped the building of the U-boat types which had been standard until that time. In their place a new class of U-boat, 245ft long, was to be constructed from pre-fabricated components. On about 18 April the launch of a U-boat of this type had been confirmed at the Schichau dockyard in Danzig, after less than 6 weeks building time on the stocks. The boat had been launched without its conning tower casing, so at that time its final shape was not known. A further 245ft boat was said to be on the stocks at Schichau. On 7 April a new vessel was observed on the stocks at Blohm & Voss, and at AG Weser in Bremen four slipways for these new boats were seen under construction. In the meantime another vessel had also been laid down there. No further information was known at this time on type designation or further characteristics of the vessels.

A few weeks later, however, another report, dated 10 June 1944, gave further details of the new U-boat type, and its type designation XXI. The report noted very good lines for high speed on the surface and under water (approximately 20 knots on the surface under diesel power, and approximately 15 knots under water with electric power). It also mentioned the large battery capacity, schnorkel, and armament of six bow torpedo tubes. Over a dozen boats were reported on the stocks, some already launched. It was thought unlikely that a substantial number would be in service by the autumn. There was no information on the production schedule.

By the autumn of 1944 very accurate information had been obtained on the overall shape and many of the characteristics of these new boats; suggested methods of locating and combatting the new vessels were already being assessed.

When Strassburg was occupied by the Allies, the entire documentation of the Strassburg Hermann Göring Werke dockyard was captured, which provided almost complete information on the new building method used for the Type XXI. This dockyard was building the basic Section 1 for the Howaldtswerke at Kiel. In the greatest possible haste these documents were taken to London, where they were translated and evaluated. By the beginning of February 1945 the Allies were in possession of detailed reports on the sequence of construction, the firms supplying parts, constructional delays and problems.

At about noon on 31 December 1944 the US airforce attacked the Blohm & Voss dockyard area with seventy-two bombers of the 8th Air Force. 948 explosive and 500 incendiary bombs were dropped, with a total weight of 187t. The slipways sustained no direct hits, but U2547 on slip 6 and U2556 on slip 10 were slightly damaged by near misses. Several high explosive bombs hit the fitting-out berths and the floating docks at the Steinwerder Bank. Here U2537 was sunk in berth 1 behind the large dockyard crane. U2530 and U2532, lying at berths 4 and 5 near the docks, sustained hits; U2532 sank altogether, while the stern of U2530 was sunk. U2515, which was in Dock V for repairs to mine damage, sustained a direct hit in Section 7.

6. The slips of the Blohm & Voss dockyard, showing seventeen Type XXI U-boats. This picture was taken at about noon on 28 October 1944 by a British reconnaissance aircraft. It shows the stern section of U2540 being towed up onto the rear part of the third slipway of building slip 9. The floating crane *Anton*, which had transported the section, is still located in front of this slipway. Amongst the other boats to be seen on the stocks are U2524 to U2539. U2524 and U2525 are visible on the second slipway of building slip 8, and are ready for launching, though still without their AA turrets. At the stern of U2525 the buoyancy vessel used for launching can be seen. The following boats – U2526 and U2527 – are on the central slipway of building slip 6. On these vessels the conning tower casing is already in place. At top left U2523 is moored; she was launched on 25 October.

7. A further British aerial photograph of the Blohm & Voss dockyard, dated 21 February 1945, showing clearly that active construction work on Type XXI U-boats was continuing, even though the Red Army was already outside Königsberg, Danzig, Küstrin and Görlitz, and in the west the fighting had reached Kleve and Saarbrücken.

It is possible to pick out sixteen Type XXI U-boats under construction on the slips (see the plan). Of these vessels, a further five had been launched by the end of the war. At the top in slip 9, the vessel is presumably U2545, shortly before her launch, and the buoyancy vessel can be seen at the stern of the boat. The vacant berths in slips 8 and 9 were earmarked for

the construction of three boats, U2562 to 2564; the sections for these vessels were subsequently towed there, and assembly begun.

In front of the unfinished and damaged liner *Vaterland* lie two Type XXI U-boats, possibly U2539 and U2540, which were commissioned at about this time.

In Docks I and IV are three Type XXI boats, and a further six at the quay. These vessels could be U2537, 2538, 2541 to 2544 and 2546 for repairs and fitting-out, and possibly U2506 and U2511, which were having final work carried out. Off the spit can be seen two Type VII C boats, possibly former training boats, being prepared for front service. Next to the large drydock Elbe

17 three Walter U-boats of the XVII B type are under construction, well camouflaged. One of them was completed, but the other two were later destroyed by bombs.

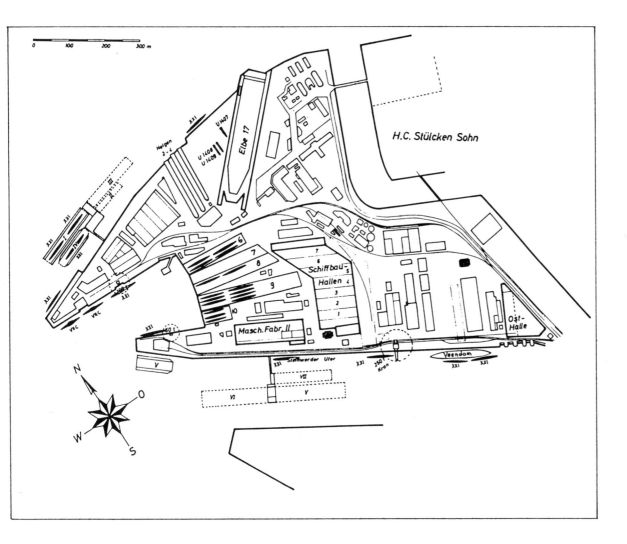

Figure 2. A sketch plan of the Blohm & Voss dockyard, identifying the U-boat types shown in the photograph opposite. Note that the large vessel at the southeastern end of the Steinwerder Bank is incorrectly identified as the barrack ship *Veendam*; it is now considered more likely that this vessel was the liner *Vaterland*, as noted in the photograph caption.

In early January 1945 the dockyard's top priority was to attempt to make good the damage in the dock area, and to repair the damaged boats up to U2537. Since the floating crane *Anton* had been severely damaged, no new boats could be towed up, with the result that new building was delayed. It was planned to repair the severely damaged Dock VII at Elbe 17, and to make good the more lightly damaged Dock V in situ. U2530 and 2532 would then be repaired in this floating dock.

A further large-scale attack on Blohm & Voss, again at about noon, on 17 January, rendered these plans impractical, however. The attack was again carried out by the 8th Air Force, with seventy-one bombers. This time 696 explosive bombs with a total weight of 174t were dropped. Several bombs fell on the slipways, and virtually all the boats were affected, with damage varying from slight to moderate: U2555 and U2556 on slip 10, U2545, 2546, 2551, 2552 and 2557 on slip 9 (most of the central slipways, which suffered the most serious damage, were vacant), U2544 on slip 8, U2542 on slip 7 and U2548 and U2550 on slip 6. To replace the unserviceable Dock VII, Dock III had been transferred to the fitting-out berths at the Steinwerder Bank. The two damaged sections of U2515 were to be removed and replaced here. The boat had already been cut up, and the new

sections were in place, but not yet welded. This was the situation when the dock was sunk by an explosive bomb. The component parts of U2515 capsized. Fourteen precious welding machines were lost, and the vessel had to be written off. The large floating Dock V, located alongside, was hit again and disintegrated. The eastern part sank, together with U2530, which had been raised in the meantime and docked there. This boat also was never repaired. At fitting-out berth 5, U2532 was being raised by the salvage ships *Hief* and *Griep* when both salvage ships were sunk by direct hits. No further salvage attempts were made. Fitting-out berth 4 was also hit; U2523, which was in that berth, was so severely damaged that it had to be decommissioned after raising.

After this, the Blohm & Voss yard was spared further air attacks, until 11 March, and it proved possible to repair much of the damage to the slipways and the boats lying there. Progress on new vessels and other work continued. After 1 February the work of towing up new boats was resumed.

The air attack on 11 March was again carried out in daytime by the 8th Air Force, whose primary target on this occasion was the oil refinery of Rhenania-Ossag. However, the eastern part of the Blohm & Voss yard was again hit, and the large 250t hammer crane suffered a direct hit, and was destroyed. U2547, which was close by after its launch, was severely damaged. In the slipway area the vacant slip 7 was hit hardest. A further bomb struck slip 9 close to U2557 and U2553, and both were damaged by bomb fragments.

The 8th Air Force struck again on 20 March, this time with only thirteen bombers, but the target this time was specifically the Blohm & Voss yard. The stern of U2550 and the adjacent seaward end of slip 6 were severely hit (see photograph 9). U2549, which was almost finished, was located behind U2550, and could not be launched as a result.

Blohm & Voss suffered further losses in Type XXI U-boats as a result of the major RAF attack on Hamburg on 9 April. More than 250 explosive bombs fell on the dockyard area, including a carpet of bombs in the area around Elbe 17. U2509 and U2514, which were being completed there, were sunk. At the construction site of the Walter U-boats next to the large dry dock, the last two Type XVII B boats, U1408 and U1409, were overturned and severely damaged by bomb hits. Of the dockyard's floating docks, only half of Dock VII was left afloat. Work on the slips was halted, and only repairs and completion work continued.

8. U2530 showing the effects of the bomb which struck her stern on 31 December 1944. The boat was due to be repaired in Dock V, but was sunk on 17 January 1945, together with the dock, during a further air attack by the 8th Air Force.

9. In a precision attack by the 8th Air Force on 20 March 1945 the stern of U2550 suffered two direct hits by 5cwt bombs.

10. U3052 at the Deschimag AG Weser yard in Bremen immediately after a devastating near miss by a 20cwt bomb on 22 February 1945. A timer fuse caused this bomb to explode about 4½m above the ground. The gigantic pressure wave pushed the bow of U3052 off the slipway and tore this part of the outer hull to shreds.

11. The same boat, U3052, 2½ months later. The destroyed outer skin panels and bow wreckage have been removed. The area of the pressure hull of Section 8 ruined by being pushed in can be seen clearly. Wooden beams prevent the leaning boat tipping over.

12. U3060 on slip 4 at Deschimag AG Weser. The sections had been towed up onto this slip in late February or early March, but had not been welded together, when Section 6 of the vessel was hit by a 5cwt bomb on 11 March. The bomb passed through the outer hull on the starboard side and detonated under the section, pushing this part out of line. Evidently further work on these boats was halted at this point. An interesting feature of all four boats on this slip is that the conning towers are absent.

13. A close-up of the effects of the bomb which struck Section 6 of U3060.

14. An aerial photograph of the AG Weser yard after the capitulation. Eight Type XXI U-boats can be seen on slip 5: at the front, from right to left, U3052, U3042, U3048 and U3056, and behind them U3053, U3043, U3049 and U3057. A near miss by a 20cwt bomb (see photograph 10) has pushed U3052 off the slipway, and the vessel leans over to port. The bow of U3042, which is lying alongside, was also seriously damaged by the same explosion, although the boat remained in position on the slipway. Presumably an emergency launch of this largely complete boat was planned, using the buoyancy vessel visible by the stern, so that the undamaged and almost finished U3043, located behind it, could be released from the stocks.

On slip 4 four U-boats can be picked out; they are U3060 (front right) and U3062 (front left), with U3061 and U3063 behind. On slip 3 the stocks for U3050 and U3051, launched on 18 and 20 April 1945, can be seen and next to them U3058 and U3059, still on the stocks.

The SU and GHG Apparatus

The most important underwater detection equipment for the Type XXI U-boat were the Gruppenhorchgerät (GHG), a listening device with forty-eight crystal receivers used for direction finding, mounted in a housing below the bow, and the 'Nibelung' SU(R) active device for direction finding and range finding of ships, using short-wave sound pulses.

The housing arrangement for the GHG receivers and the SU(R) apparatus had been planned in 1943 as a development for earlier submarines, and was then adopted for the Type XXI. The arrangement of the GHG housing under the forestem was a technically simple solution. However, tests showed interference due to eddying around poorly designed and fitted components. The shape of the housing, designed from the point of view of simplicity of production, was also unsatisfactory. A new profile was introduced later, which was better in terms of streamlining, and brought an improvement in this area.

In order to provide swift and reliable recognition of loud or particularly distinctive sounds (eg torpedoes) at close range, one receiver on either side of the GHG housing was connected to a three-stage amplifier system, which in turn fed loudspeakers in the conning tower and the listening room. By selectively switching the two receivers on and off, it was possible to monitor the entire horizon, or determine the side on which a detected noise source lay. This device was known as the NHG(L) (Nautisches Horchgerät mit Lautsprechern).

The latest type of active underwater direction finding device (S-apparatus) which the German navy had available in late 1943 was the SZ system, which was intended to serve as a stop-gap measure for surface ships until the 'Nothung' SR device, intended to be the eventual solution, could be introduced. Ten of these SZ devices were modified for use in U-boats. In this guise they were given the code name S-Mi ('Mine'). They were the starting point for the development of the SU(R), or S-device for U-boats with a Braun-type display tube.

After spring 1944 S-Mi devices were installed and tested in a number of Type VII C U-boats. Tactical testing of the units began in November 1944 on U393 and U1008 in the Sultan experimental group. The new 'Nibelung' SU(R) device, planned for the Type XXI, incorporated several innovations: the oscillating base was to be sited in a new position on the forward edge of the conning tower, and important parts of the receiving system were also new. As a result it became clear by early 1944 that the first forty Type XXI boats would be commissioned without this direction finding device. The manufacture of the supplementary equipment, whose pur-

pose was to record the pulse echo automatically, turned out to be even more problematic. This apparatus consisted of the Carpentia recorder, which made marks on electrolytic paper, and the Sarotti device, which was intended to produce a panoramic image of the echo on the screen of a sighting device. In fact, it proved impossible to develop these items of equipment to an operationally reliable state before the end of the war.

Another passive close-range direction-finding device, the SP apparatus, operated in conjunction with parts of an SU receiver system. This installation was intended to complement an underwater rocket ('Ursel') armament system, which was to be installed in the stern of the Type XXI U-boat, but it failed to progress beyond the testing stage (on U38, U393 and U1008).

It was not until the end of 1944 that the first Nibelung units were installed on Type XXI U-boats. At about this time a special U-flotilla (the 18th) was established in Gotenhafen, whose purpose was to train personnel in the use of this new direction finding equipment. The theoretical tuition took place on the accommodation ship *Walter Rau*, and the on-board training on U1161, U1162, UD4 and UA, ie not on Type XXI boats. Of these U-boats, some had S-equipment on board, including at least U1162 and UD4. The training courses for Oberfunkmeister (master radio operators) lasted 14 days.

The first systematic testing of the 'water sound systems' SU(R) and GHG in Type XXI U-boats was carried out using U2506 off Pillau in late December 1944. On 28 December 1944, with a force 5–6 westerly wind and swell 4, interference levels affecting the SU apparatus were measured, with the boat at periscope depth. At moderately high speeds a fairly high level of interference was recorded in the straight-ahead direction, which was due to the flooding hole above the rotating base of the SU, the loosely fitting sheet metal housing, and possibly also to the barrels of the 2cm AA guns. Interference levels were at a minimum in the transverse directions, but then increased again towards the aft direction. The cause was again thought to be the loose-fitting casing, which revealed gaps 1cm wide. The level of interference aft to port was higher than to starboard, due to the port location of the fog horn. These results were obtained both under electric power and using the schnorkel, although interference levels were slightly higher overall using the schnorkel.

Before range tests with the SU system were carried out, on 29 December 1944, the upper flooding hole was temporarily sealed. The result was that perfect direction finding results were obtained even at 200 revolutions (11 knots), from forward to about 110 degrees aft on both sides (at lower speeds up to 140 degrees). Using the *Donau*, steaming at 10 knots, as a target, the system provided reliable direction finding at a range of 8000m on several approaches at 200 revolutions. In terms of accuracy, a maximum direction finding error of + or – 1.5 degrees was achieved, measured against bearings taken by periscope.

At the same time that the Nibelung testing was in progress, work continued on the GHG. Under similar conditions – running at 200 revolutions, against the *Donau* – a maximum range of about 8000m was also obtained with this equipment. Measurements of interference levels affecting the GHG showed that the method of mounting the receivers in the housing was unsatisfactory. It was also clear that streamlining suffered from the effects of housing plate joint lines, and from projecting screw heads. At speeds of 170 revolutions and above the GHG suffered higher levels of interference under water than on the surface. This indicated that the conning tower casing and the upper deck, with its many openings, were poorly designed from the point of view of streamlining.

Attempts were made to rectify these shortcomings as far as possible when it was time to test the system in U3504. The housing round the rotary base of the SU was welded up tight on all sides, and all welding seams were ground smooth. A bar located below the housing was removed, and the flooding hole above the base sealed. No changes were made to the GHG housing. When examined later in dock, however, the housing made a more favourable impression than that on U2506. The only complaint was that the transition from forestem to housing was unsatisfactory from the point of view of streamlining, that thick welding fillets were evident, and that some of the putty which was used to fair the joint seams had fallen out.

On 9 and 10 January 1945 interference levels, direction finding and range finding were measured on U3504, north of Hela. Although the results of the interference tests were better, the direction finding and range measurements were unsatisfactory. Conditions for listening and direction finding were poor (severe close-range echoing at about 1000–1500m), and in consequence the SU device was only able to achieve reliable indications of the *Donau* at ranges up to 3000m. With the GHG, the range limit was 4000m. The direction finding accuracy achieved with the GHG was about 1 degree higher on average than with the SU device, the hand-driven rotating base of which exhibited up to about 3 degrees of slack.

The Nibelung system was subsequently tested on a convoy of thirteen vessels, together with a further Type XXI U-boat which had in the meantime been equipped with the SU device.

By the end of the war it was said that eighty SU sets had been produced for the Type XXI. Whether they were all installed is another matter. It is certain, however, that all boats planned for operational service were fitted with this system during the final fitting-out stage.

In March 1945 at AG Weser the GHG housing of the NVK experimental boat U3003 was fitted with a 3mm thick streamlined sheet metal housing which was permeable to sound. The new housing provided a listening range of 3–4nm even at speeds of 13–15.5 knots. This shroud never, however, became a standard fitting.

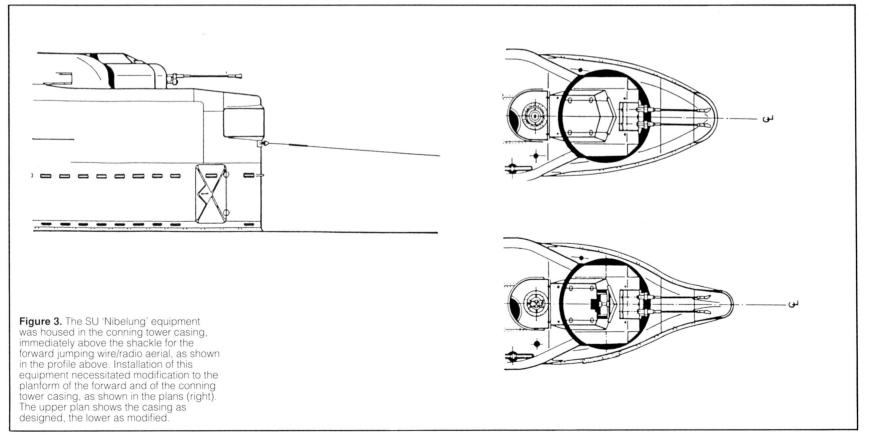

Figure 3. The SU 'Nibelung' equipment was housed in the conning tower casing, immediately above the shackle for the forward jumping wire/radio aerial, as shown in the profile above. Installation of this equipment necessitated modification to the planform of the forward and of the conning tower casing, as shown in the plans (right). The upper plan shows the casing as designed, the lower as modified.

BIBLIOGRAPHICAL NOTE

Eberhard Rössler, co-author of this volume in the Anatomy series, is widely regarded as an authority on German U-boats. Further details about the Type XXI may be found in the following works, of which he is also the author:

U-Boottyp XXI 1st edn Munich 1967, 4th edn Koblenz 1986

Geschichte des deutschen U-Bootbaus 1st edn Munich 1974, 2nd edn (vol 2) Koblenz 1987

'The Legendary XXI's' *Aviation and Marine International* 34, 35, 37, 38, Lugano, 1976

Die deutschen U-Boote und ihre Werften 1st edn (vol 2) Munich 1980, 2nd edn Koblenz 1990

The U-boat London and Melbourne 1981

Die Torpedos der deutschen U-Boote Herford 1984

'Erprobungs-Unterseeboot *Wilhelm Bauer*' *Deutsches Schiffahrtsarchiv* Bremerhaven 7/1984

Vom Original zum Modell: Uboottyp XXI Koblenz 1988

An article in the guide to the Technikmuseum *Wilhelm Bauer* on the history of the Type XII, Bremerhaven 1990

Die Sonaranlagen der deutschen U-Boote Herford 1991

The Photographs

15. A superbly sharp stern view of the Type XXI U-boat. This is U2502, photographed in Britain after the war.

16. A view from the surface control station of the bow of U3037. The two barrels of the forward 2cm AA turret are in the foreground. The large opening in the nose of the conning tower casing indicates that the base of the Nibelung underwater detection apparatus has not yet been installed.

18. The conning tower casing of U3037. The identification symbol under the slot for the starboard navigation lamp indicates that the boat is still in UAK condition. The large yellow recognition stripes were carried by all training boats.

Aft of the mast with the German ensign the extended mattress aerial for the FuMO 61 Hohentwiel radar and radar detection equipment can be seen. On the starboard side the conning tower casing is belled out slightly to accommodate the retracted schnorkel head. On the schnorkel head itself is the wide-band Bali panoramic receiver aerial, operating over 100–400MHz. With this detection aerial short wave reception was possible even when the schnorkel was in use. With the schnorkel retracted, the Bali aerial projected out of the bridge roof, as can be seen here, and could therefore also be used when the U-boat was on the surface.

17. The forward part of U3504's conning tower casing. Her commander, Kptl Karl-Hartwig Siebold, joined the navy in 1936, the year of the Berlin Olympic Games; the officer class of that year adopted the Olympic rings (visible here) as their unofficial symbol. The housing for the rotating Nibelung sonar (SU) equipment, which was tested extensively on 9 and 10 January 1945, can be seen above the Olympic rings insignia.

19. U2524 after the completion of operational training in April 1945, at the Flender works at Lübeck. On 3 May 1945 the boat was with U2540, U3030 and U3032, adjacent to the escort ship *Bolkoburg* of the 25th U-Flotilla, south of Fehmarn. In a series of British air attacks on this group of ships U3032 was sunk and *Bolkoburg* set on fire; U2540 and U3030 escaped undamaged. U2524 was also unharmed, but was eventually scuttled off Fehmarn.

20. (Above right) U2506 in early May 1945, at Bergen, Norway. This boat (Kptl Horst von Schroeter) had put to sea from Kiel on 14 April 1945, carrying the Chief of the KIU U-boat design division, Ministerialrat (Ministry Advisor) Aschmoneit. During a deep diving test on 26 April, the vessel had reached a depth of 220m. She then made a passage to Bergen via Kristiansand, where she was due to prepare for operational service at the front. On 17 May, before she became operational, U2506 was taken over by the British, who transported her to Lisahally on 14 June.

U2511, to the right of U2506, had put to sea on patrol on 30 April. This mission had to be broken off four days later, however, when a ban on submarine attacks was ordered.

The Type XXI boats U2506, U2511 and U3514, handed over to the British at Bergen, never saw service again. They were sunk during Operation Deadlight, northeast of Ireland, 1–3 January 1946.

21. U2506 at Kristiansand on 28 April 1945. The picture shows the departure of Ministerialrat Aschmoneit.

22. The conning towers of two Type XXI U-boats sunk at Bremen.

In the foreground is the tower of U3036, with half-extended schnorkel and the hydraulically extended periscope support for both periscopes. The AA turrets are missing. This boat had been launched on 27 January 1945. According to the schedule, the auxiliary machinery was due to be tested in early February, followed by static testing of the diesel engines and the main electric motors. On 6 February trim testing was to be completed, and finally, after the installation of double 3cm mounts, final testing was due to start on 9 February. Subsequent to this, the boat would stay in dock from 10 to 13 February. After final cleaning and painting, U 3036 was due to commission on 20 February. In fact this schedule proved impossible. The boat was still in AG Weser's Floating Dock V on 25 February, when the dock was severely damaged in an air attack; U3036 capsized. After salvage, she was towed to the fitting-out pier for repairs, and was sunk there on 30 March when hit by bombs.

The roof of the bridge of a second Type XXI boat projects out of the water on the night. It shows the extended sky or navigation periscope and the Hohentwiel mattress antenna of the FuMO 61, together with AA turrets minus their barrels. The circular opening forward of the aft AA turret in the bridge roof may have been made for the wide-angle navigation periscope. This U-boat is U3046, also sunk on 30 March.

23. A further Type XXI U-boat sunk at Bremen. This is U3045, which sank on 30 March. U3045 and U3046 had already completed their acceptance trials, and bore the yellow identification stripe of the training U-boat, visible in this picture.

24. The conning towers of two Type XXI boats, U2547 and U3502, projecting out of the water; they were scuttled on 3 May 1945 at a mooring pontoon at Tollerort, Hamburg. U3502 (probably the boat without AA turrets) had been taken out of service after being struck by a bomb in the stern compartment on 8 April, after which time it served only as a power supply vessel.

25. U2501 in May 1945, in front of the Elbe II U-boat bunker at the Howaldtswerke yard at Hamburg. With her large electrical installation the boat was able to provide power for the bunker in March and April 1945, while repairs and other work were being carried out on U-boats due for front service. The sole officer on board during this period was Oblt Ing Noack, who scuttled the boat on 3 May 1945 at 7 o'clock outside the entrance to the Western Basin. As well as the stern of U2501, the wreck (bow and conning tower) of an incomplete Type VII C boat (presumably U685, built by Howaldt) can be seen.

26. On 9 September 1944 U3503 became the third Type XXI boat built by Schichau in Danzig to be commissioned. In October this boat was the subject of extensive type testing in the Danzig UAK area. Training for operational service then began, but had to be interrupted for repairs at the Holm dockyard in Danzig, and for antenna testing at the NEK off Stolpmünde. In the end, training was not completed until 7 March 1945, at the Agru Front-Hela.

Between 1 and 20 April completion work was carried out at the Howaldtswerke at Hamburg, but the work was restricted to 'the most essential repairs and equipment, due to the urgency of the position'. After 22 April the boat was at Kiel, fitting-out for front service. In early May she put to sea with other boats, making for Norway.

On 6 May U3503 suffered minor damage through near-misses by bombs. The boat then entered Swedish territorial waters, and was captured by the Swedish destroyer *Norrköping*. The stern had been flooded by the U-boat crew, as a pretence of more serious damage, and constant pumping was necessary to keep her afloat.

On 8 May the Swedish ship received instructions to relax her watch on the U-boat, and U3503 subsequently sank stern-first. Presumably the crew had ceased pumping.

The picture shows U3503 still flying the German ensign. The crew has assembled on the upper deck with their belongings, while the stern is already awash.

27. Cleaning work being carried out on U3017 at the Horten U-boat base after the weapons had fallen silent – a short-lived idyll. Behind her are U3041 and U2502. On 20 May these boats were taken over by the British at Oslo, and they were transported to the Lisahally U-boat collection point in Northern Ireland in early June.

28. U3008 at Kiel in late May 1945, flying the British flag. The boat had put to sea from Wilhelmshaven shortly before the end of the war, under the command of Kptl Helmut Manseck, and was due to operate from Bergen. At the time of the capitulation the boat was located off southern Norway. In defiance of the British instruction to deliver the boat to England, Kptl Manseck steered the boat through the German minefields to Frederikshavn, Denmark. From there he continued along the Danish coast to Kiel, where he anchored on 25 May. U3008 was then taken to Wilhelmshaven, and then to Lisahally on 25 June. There she was transferred to the US Navy, who took her to the USA in August 1945.

29. Type XXI U-boats at Lisahally; in the foreground, from left to right, U2502, U3514 and U2518, behind them U2506, U2511 and U3041. U3017, which had originally been part of this group, has already been taken away. The picture therefore could not have been taken before August 1945. Of these boats, U3041 was assigned to the USSR and U2518 to France. The other boats were sunk in the North Atlantic in early 1946 by the British (Operation Deadlight).

30. The after part of the conning tower casing of U2502, showing the AA turret. A circular opening is visible in the bridge roof to the left of the AA turret, through which the hydraulic rod aerial projects. This picture was taken at Lisahally.

31. Six surrendered Type XXI boats at Lisahally in the summer of 1945. In the foreground is the roof of the bridge of U3017 with the recesses for the bridge watch. The speaking tubes are clearly visible, as are the extended armoured panels which were intended for protection against gunfire and also provided protection against wind and spray. Alongside U3017 are U2518 (left) and U2502 (right). Ahead of U2518, the stern of U3515 is visible, and alongside her are U2529 and U3514.

32. A view of slips 9 and 10 at the Blohm & Voss yard, Hamburg, at the end of the war. On slip 10 in the background to the left are (left to right) U2557, U2556 and U2555, with U2563 and U2561 nearest the water on slip 9. In the foreground, on the second rank building stocks in slip 9, are U2564, U2562 and U2560. These uncompleted boats are being inspected by British servicemen.

33. The Deschimag AG Weser yard at Bremen at the end of the war, from a slightly different angle from that shown in the frontispiece of this book. U3052, pushed off the building stocks by a bomb near miss on 22 February 1945, can be seen leaning to port on the extreme left.

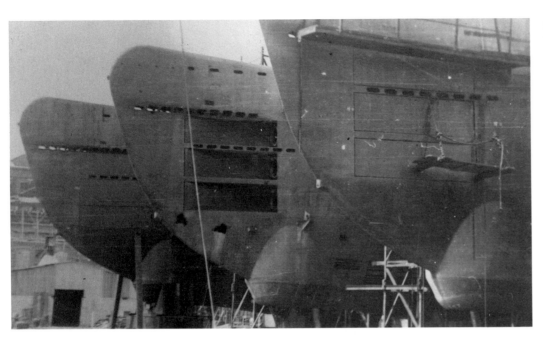

34. The bows of (left to right) U2564, U2562 and U2560 at the landward end of the second rank of building stocks on slip 9 at the Blohm & Voss yard at Hamburg at the end of the war.

35. Above right: Partly completed central control sections manufactured by the Howaldtswerke at Hamburg. In contrast to the section 5s made in Vegesack and Danzig, the conning towers were already mounted on these sections, together with periscope brackets.

36. Another view of the bows of U2564, U2562 and U2560, uncompleted on slip 9 at Blohm & Voss, Hamburg, at the end of the war.

37. Lt Cdr A D Piper RNR and Lt P C Chapman RN inspecting the torpedo room of U3008 towards the end of May 1945, while the boat was still at Kiel. To the left are the controls for the low-noise compressed air ejection system for the port tubes.

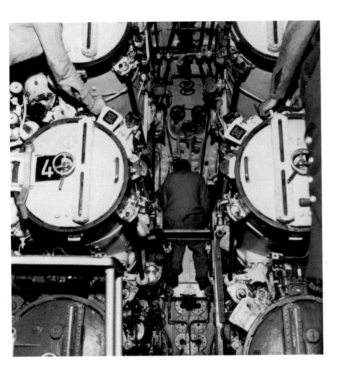

38. The torpedo tube installation of U2518 in the hands of a French crew after the boat had been transferred to France. An operator can be seen sitting in front of the LUT adjustor device, between the tubes.

39. Section 1 of a Type XXI U-boat, with the rudder not yet in place. In the background is a Section 3, seen from aft.

40. U2502 was originally allotted to the Royal Navy for test purposes, but the vessel proved unsuitable due to engine damage, and in its place U3017 (British designation N 41) was selected for the same purpose. But here too the the RN were unlucky. During an inspection of U3017 at the Vickers dockyard at Barrow on 29 August a battery explosion occurred, which postponed the planned tests again. In late 1949 U3017 was scrapped. The picture shows U3017 (N 41) in England.

41. On 24 August 1946, U3503 was raised by the Swedish navy, examined closely, and finally broken up. The picture shows U3503 after raising, in a floating dock at the Göta dockyard.

42. U3503's conning tower during breaking-up operations, already without its casing. From forward to aft are: the UZO (torpedo aiming) column, the circular radio direction finding aerial, the conning tower hatch, pipes for the extending mast of the radio rangefinding apparatus (FuMO 61 radar), the air exhaust and the rod aerial. The periscope bracket has already been removed.

43. U2540 after raising, with the conning tower casing already removed. From left to right are the guide tube for the retractable rod aerial, the air exhaust and the outer schnorkel pipe. In the foreground is the opening for the galley hatch.

44. In late August 1945, after crossing the Atlantic, U3008 entered the US navy base of New London (Conn). Leaving New London, the vessel arrived at Portsmouth (NH) on 13 September, where she was extensively overhauled and tested. These procedures were not completed until summer 1946. One of the new features of the boat was a new conning tower casing devoid of AA turrets. On 24 July 1946 the boat was commissioned for a second time under Cdr Everett H Steinmetz, and subsequently assigned to the 2nd Submarine Squadron, in which she operated off the coast of New England until March 1947.

On 31 March 1947 U3008 was transferred to the Operational Development Force in Key West, Florida. On the way there the boat stayed in Norfolk for three weeks. On 23 April U3008 entered Key West, where she joined the 4th Submarine Squadron. After extensive testing, the purpose of which was the development of a new submarine and new submarine combat tactics, the boat returned to New London in October 1947, where she stayed over the winter of 1947–48. After this, U3008 returned to Key West in order to resume the testing programme, which lasted until June 1948. The submarine was no longer needed, and on 18 June 1948 she was taken out of service at Portsmouth. For a further period of several years U3008 was used for technical testing, and it was not until 1955 that she was released for scraping, and sold off on 15 September 1955. She was broken up in 1956.

45. U2518 with extended hydroplanes on 23 March 1946 in a drydock at Cherbourg. At the time this U-boat was on loan to France.

46. A view of the remains of the wreck of U3004. The conning tower mantle can be made out, cut off just above the hull. The opening of the conning tower hatch is clearly visible, together with the stump of the sky or navigation periscope and finally the shaft for an elevator periscope, which was tested on this boat. The other stumps projecting from the hull aft of the conning tower belong to the schnorkel (front) and the aerials (rear). The conning tower casing visible behind U3004 belongs to U3506.

These boats, brought in for repairs, were scuttled by crew members on 3 May 1945, together with U2505, in the West Basin of the Elbe II U-boat bunker. Later, when the U-boat bunker was demolished by order of the British, the concrete roof partially collapsed, burying these boats. In the early 1950s an attempt was made to dismantle for scrap the U-boats located under the rubble, as far as they were accessible at low tide. However, it proved possible only to reach the sterns and superstructures. The remaining vessels were forgotten until 1986–87, when they were rediscovered through the research and painstaking investigations of the U-boat researchers Jak P Mallmann-Showell and Walter Cloots.

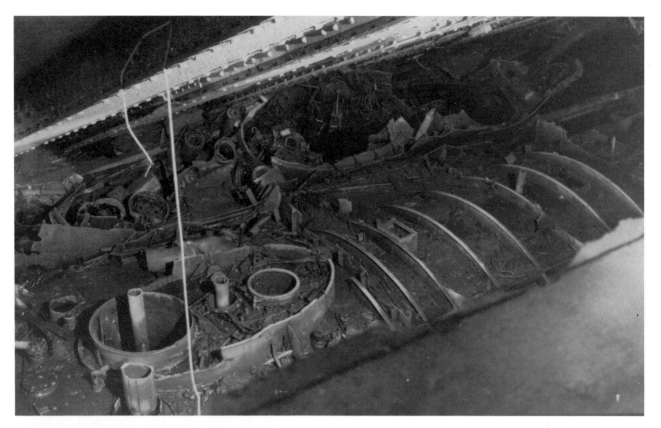

47. A view of the stern of *U-Wilhelm Bauer* after she had undergone an overhaul for the Technical Museum in the spring of 1984. The after hydroplanes and the fixed stabiliser surfaces with three-bladed propellers can be seen forward of the large rudder.

48. The original hydraulic rudder system of U3001.

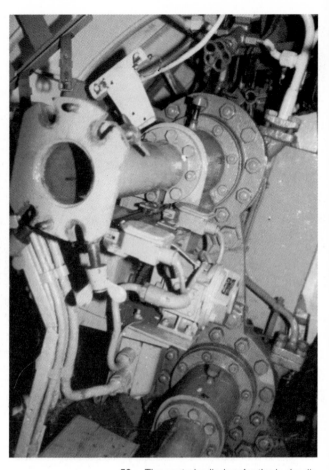

50. The control cylinders for the hydraulic rudder (top) and hydroplane (bottom) system. This system was re-installed in *U-Wilhelm Bauer* with virtually no modifications.

49. A view into the stern compartment of a No 1 section; on the left is the aft bulkhead wall of the after WC, in the centre the lathe, on the right two large high pressure air bottles, and above them the starter for deep bilge pump No 1, which is not yet in place, and the valves for this bilge pump. Underneath in the stern compartment bilges are the foundations for the WC cesspit tanks.

52. A replacement cooling water pump (identical to the shallow bilge pump in the 'pump cellar') with its associated starter on the port side of the bulkhead to the stern compartment. Adjacent to it on the right is the port propeller shaft, and above it the rear bearing of the port main electric motor.

51. The Asdic decoy ejector on the starboard outer wall of the stern room of U2518. This was used to eject decoys under water, to provide a diversionary target for enemy Asdic.

54. A view from the stern compartment to the electric motor room hatch. Next to the hatch on the right-hand side is the door to the after WC, on the left the deep bilge pump No 1, above it the piston for opening and closing the airlock located above the stern compartment. The pipe for filling and draining the airlock, with a slight glass, is on the right, next to the WC compartment.

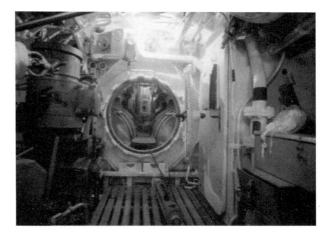

53. Deep bilge pump No 1 on the port side of the stern compartment of *U-Wilhelm Bauer*. At top left is the flooding valve for the diver's airlock and at top right the handwheel for the bulkhead slider controlling the air inlet duct to the stern compartment. In front of the pump are the drain hose from the airlock and a depth gauge.

56. A main electric motor, type 2 GU 365/30, from a Type XXI (this example from U2540) opened up for a refit at Siemens-Schuckert, Hamburg.

57. The switch panel above the port silent running motor of a Type XXI U-boat.

55. The electric motor room, showing the main electric motors (made by Siemens), with the large air coolers above them. In the background is the pressure-tight bulkhead to the stern compartment.

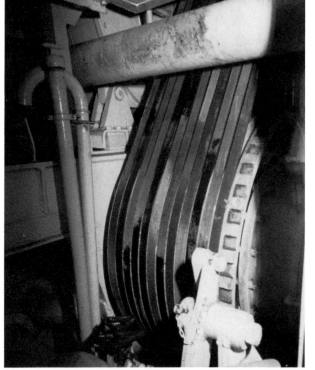

58. The V-belt drive system for the port silent running motor. The system of twelve V-belts reduces motor speed in the ratio 2.68:1. Power is transmitted to the main shaft via a friction clutch.

Using this silent running motor system the Type XXI U-boats could achieve 6 knots under water in virtual silence. On earlier U-boats this speed could only be achieved with their electric motors switched to full speed, which was accompanied by a high level of noise. Operating under these circumstances, the old boats provided a good target for enemy listening systems. In contrast, the US Navy carried out listening tests on U2513 in late 1946, after they had received the vessel as a prize, and they found that they could not locate the boat reliably when it was running silently even at a range of only 220m.

61. A view from forward of both control panels for the main electric motors in *U-Wilhelm Bauer*. The casings were colour coded red for port, green for the starboard side.

59. The starboard electric motor panel in *U-Wilhelm Bauer*. It was reconstructed from the port electric motor panel formerly fitted in U2540. Under the instruments are: on the left, a revolutions counter; on the right, the resistance regulator; in the centre, the large handwheel switch; and below that the change-over rocker switch for selecting forward or reverse.

60. The starboard side of the large motor control station in the forward part of the electric motor room of *U-Wilhelm Bauer*. In the centre is the new monitor panel for the silent-running motors, next to it on the extreme left is the automatic diesel monitor, and above that an exhaust gas pressure gauge. On the far right is the handwheel switch for the starboard electric motor panel.

63. On the port side next to the bulkhead door leading to the diesel compartment are the two diesel engine monitor panels, and below them the starter for the gearbox oil pump. On the right were the large switch box with the two starter handwheels for the new electric compressors made by Poppe and the generator switch panel.

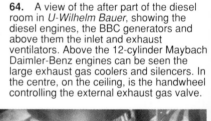

64. A view of the after part of the diesel room in *U-Wilhelm Bauer*, showing the diesel engines, the BBC generators and above them the inlet and exhaust ventilators. Above the 12-cylinder Maybach Daimler-Benz engines can be seen the large exhaust gas coolers and silencers. In the centre, on the ceiling, is the handwheel controlling the external exhaust gas valve.

62. The fuel header tank above the control stand on *U-Wilhelm Bauer*. Two engine telegraphs are attached to it. Above them on the left is the handwheel for the rapid-closure valve for the header tank, and on the right the actuator for the outer exhaust gas flap. In the centre, in front of the tank is the handwheel for the battery transfer switch.

65. The new diesel engine installation in *U-Wilhelm Bauer*, showing the port MB 820 S1 engine made by Maybach Daimler-Benz, a high-speed 12-cylinder unit, producing 600hp at 1400rpm. In front of the engine is a BBC generator rated at 450kW (950 A and 400 V at 1440rpm), with the suction duct for the air cooling system. The pipework above the large silencer and engine exhaust gas cooler is the outlet from the battery rooms to the engine's inlet filter. On the port side (background right) lies the air purification system, with its containers of potash to remove carbon dioxide from the air.

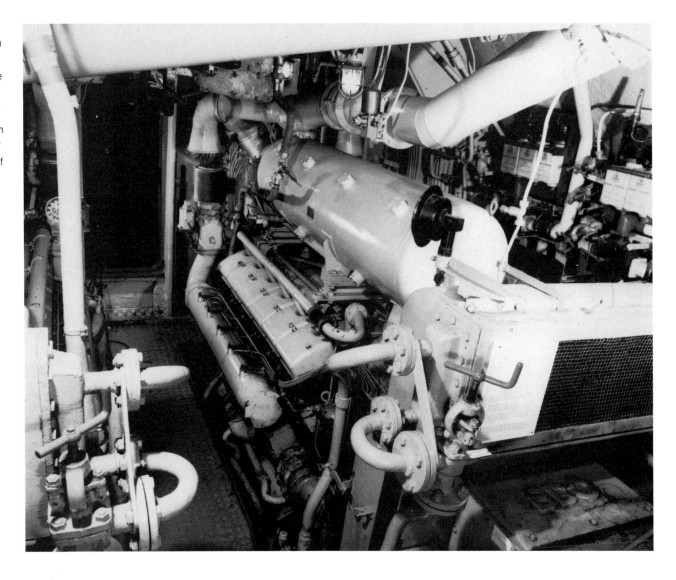

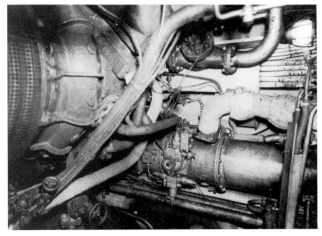

66. The after end of the diesel room on U2518; on the left is the Büchi exhaust gas fan for the starboard diesel engine, behind it the starboard Junkers compressor. U2518 was the only Type XXI boat surrendered to Britain which was still fitted with this overflow supercharger fan for the diesel engines. In the centre of the air compressor the heavily insulated exhaust pipe branches off. The pipes under the compressor are air coolers.

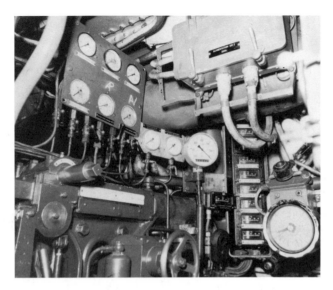

67. The port diesel control station on U2518. On the right, next to the air inlet handwheel, are the exhaust gas temperature gauges and an engine telegraph.

69. The starboard ventilator (air inlet) with its connection to the air inlet selector switch, and a branch pipe running to the circulation ventilator and the air purification system. Below is the desk for the starboard diesel control station. On the right are the valves for the fuel transfer system, including the sighting glass and pressure gauge.

70. A view into a section 4 from aft; above is the central passage with the crew's accommodation on either side, and below the port and starboard battery compartments 2.1, with an inspection passage running between. In the bottom battery room 1.1 the rails for the roof-mounted inspection carriage are clearly visible.

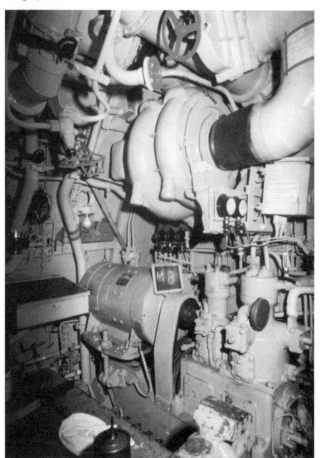

68. The starboard ventilator (air inlet) above the new Poppe III/2 air compressor in the forward part of the diesel room in *U-Wilhelm Bauer*.

73. The large electric compressor (air compressor No 3) on the port side of the auxiliary machinery room ('pump cellar') of *U-Wilhelm Bauer*. This is the original HK 1.5 compressor made by Krupp-GW (built in 1944), which could provide compressed air at 200 atmospheres at a rate of 16l/min.

71. A view aft into the port after living quarters of *U-Wilhelm Bauer*, which are still largely as they would have looked in an original Type XXI.

72. The starboard side of the 'pump cellar', with the shallow bilge pump at the rear right. Behind the ladder to the central control room the valves for the regulating tanks and regulating bunkers can be seen, and in front of them an inner stopcock for flooding and emptying, and at bottom left the valves for the emergency emptying of the battery rooms.

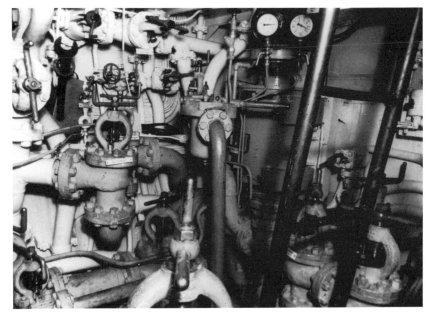

74. A view into the 'pump cellar' of *U-Wilhelm Bauer*. On the left in the background is the shallow bilge pump, in front of it the filter for fine flooding, the contents gauge for the regulating cells and adjacent on the right the valve for flooding and emptying the regulating cells. On the extreme right is the air inlet distributor for the regulating cells.

75. The forward end of the 'pump cellar' on a Type XXI U-boat, with the battery ventilator (top left) and the deep bilge pump No 2 (in the background).

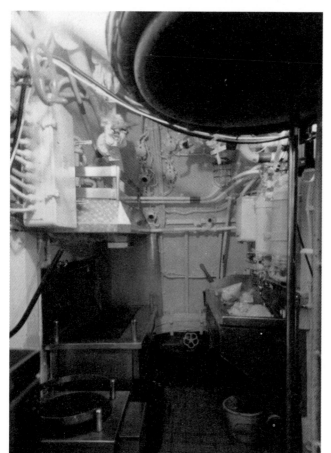

76. The galley of *U-Wilhelm Bauer*, on the port side of the galley hatch to the conning tower casing. On the left is a 50-litre boiler, with an electric stove and extractor behind it. The handwheel controls the bulkhead valve for the air inlet duct. On the opposite side are two sinks, with the carbon filter for the drinking water system above them.

77. The outer pipe of the schnorkel in the rear part of the central control room of a Type XXI U-boat. Adjacent to it on the left is auxiliary switch panel No 2, above it the valve for the internal stop-cock for draining the schnorkel, and next to it on the right, the handwheel for operating the exhaust air valve.

79. The port side of the central control room of *U-Wilhelm Bauer*. Above the switches for the exciter transformer can be seen the Nereus echograph, made by Atlas. Behind it are the control apparatus and sighting device for the radar system.

78. The hydroplane stations of *U-Wilhelm Bauer*. Above the forward hydroplane station (left) are the depth gauges (up to 25m, up to 400m, and the Papenberg manometer). Above the after hydroplane station is the mechanical rudder position indicator and the trim gauge. Next to them on the right is the housing for the automatic hydroplane system, and above the housing are the boxes bearing the indicator lamps for the vessel's stopcocks. The electric rudder position indicators (made by Tuschka) are located in the rectangular boxes with the dark scale background on the right of the forward hydroplane station and above the after control station.

80. On the port side of the forward central control room bulkhead are the two pressure oil pumps for the hydraulic system. Below them the trim system can be seen, with two handwheels controlling the compressed air trimming system. At bottom left is a manually operated oil supply pump, and on the right the pressure oil filter, standing at an angle. On the left, next to the pressure oil pumps, is *U-Wilhelm Bauer*'s new echograph made by Atlas, mounted on the wall of the pressure hull.

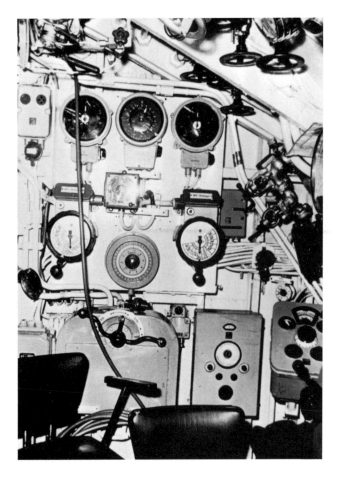

81. The rudder station in the central control room of *U-Wilhelm Bauer*. Above the steering lever (rocker) are two further engine telegraphs and two revolutions gauges, and between them a repeater compass and the rudder indicator. On the far right, in the corner, is the control desk for the automatic rudder system made by Anschütz/Tuschka. The master gyro compass formerly located here has been shifted to the front port side of the auxiliary machinery room on *U-Wilhelm Bauer*. Above the rudder station are the valves for the diesel exhaust system.

83. The periscope in the conning tower of *U-Wilhelm Bauer*. At top right is the extender switch (slider) located to port of the hydraulic periscope system.

82. The conning tower casing of *U-Wilhelm Bauer* with the distinctive yellow identification stripe of this experimental civilian U-boat.

84. The surface control station in the forward part of the conning tower of *U-Wilhelm Bauer*, showing the rudder station for surface running, a repeater compass, two engine telegraphs, two revolutions indicators and one rudder indicator. On the left is the alarm button, and on the right the ladder to the bridge.

86. The after part of the surface control station of *U-Wilhelm Bauer*, showing the opening (above) for the bridge watch. Behind it is the periscope housing.

87. A view from the protected surface control station of *U-Wilhelm Bauer* in Kiel harbour.

85. The swivel and tilt base of the M1H sonar in the forward part of the conning tower casing of *U-Wilhelm Bauer*. It is mounted in a 1.2m high dome, and can be serviced from inside the pressure hull. It is a panoramic system with approximately 4kW pulse power.

89. The conning tower casing of *U-Wilhelm Bauer* in Autumn 1983, after the vessel had been handed over to the study/research group of the German Maritime Museum in Bremerhaven. Unfortunately this cladding was removed during the overhaul, and replaced by a non-standard version. It is planned to install a reconstructed Type XXI conning tower casing to the museum boat at some stage although this will not match the internal fittings of *U-Wilhelm Bauer*.

90. The control panels for the GHG (left) and the Nibelung SU equipment (right) on the forward bulkhead of the listening room on U2518. Above them are the revolutions gauge and a repeater compass. In the Type XXI U-boat the opposite, rear, bulkhead of the listening room was fitted with the controls and instruments for the Hohentwiel system.

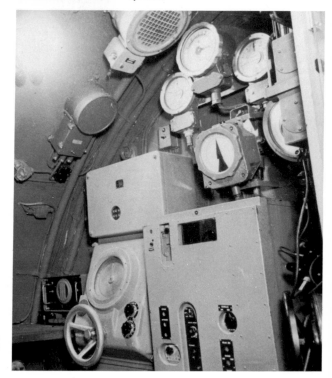

88. The schnorkel head of U2513, fitted with glued-on radar-absorbent Wesch mats. This protective measure against short wave radar radiation reduced reflection in the 9cm range to about 30 per cent.

92. A close-up of the Type XXI's schnorkel head without anti-radar Wesch mats.

91. The starboard test room of *U-Wilhelm Bauer* after her conversion. On the outer wall from right to left are the GHG compensator, the emergency gyro compass, and above it the power supply and distribution panel. In the background the control device for the M1H sonar system can be seen.

93. A view into the washroom of *U-Wilhelm Bauer*. On the left are three wash basins, and behind them a foot bath, a further wash basin and above it a water heater. Adjacent on the right is the shower.

94. A view from aft into the torpedo magazine of U2518. On the left, next to the aftmost support arm, the electric motors for transverse movement of the torpedo cradles can be seen. In the background the inner doors of the torpedo tubes can be made out.

95. The hydraulic extension mechanism for the forward hydroplanes on U2518.

98. The housing for the sonar equipment (GHG) of U2549 on slip 6 of the Blohm & Voss yard at Hamburg. The sharp angle between the forestem and the trough-shaped housing, which proved to have a marked effect on streamlining, is clearly visible. Steel brackets are welded to the forestem above the housing, so that this projecting part of the ship can be supported on the stock.

96. A view from forward into a No 7 section, showing the torpedo magazine. This section was built by the Seebeck dockyard at Wesermünde.

97. The torpedo system of *U-Wilhelm Bauer*, reduced to four tubes. The upper tubes are the original design used in the Type XXI U-boat, but the lower ones were installed as Ablauf tubes; they are longer, and of slightly larger diameter.

99. The bow of *U-Wilhelm Bauer* in Autumn 1983. Clearly visible is the front end of the new 7.5m Ablauf torpedo tube, projecting slightly out of the external skin. Below it is the sealed lower torpedo door, the GHG housing, and aft of that the recess containing the patent anchor.

The Drawings

A General arrangement and external appearance

A1/1

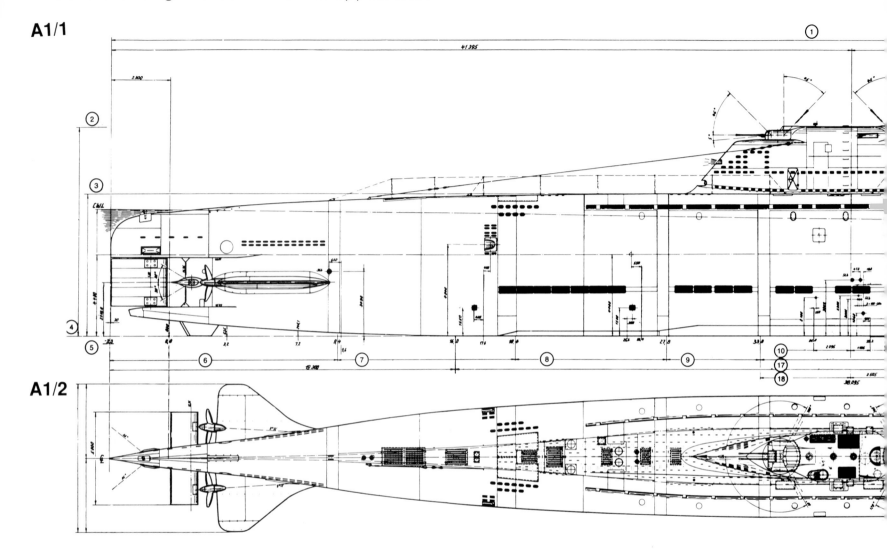

A1/2

A1/3

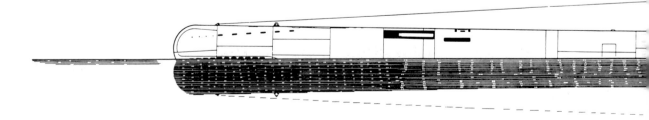

A1   **TYPE XXI AS DESIGNED (1944)**
      (1/200 scale)

A1/1   **Starboard elevation**

A1/2   **Plan**

A1/3   **Waterline elevation (port side)**

1   Length overall 76.700m
2   Height to top of conning tower
     11.344m
3   Height to upper deck 7.700m
4   Base line (keel sole)
5   Frame stations
6   Section 1 length 12.700m
7   Section 2 length 10.000m
8   Section 3 length 8.400m
9   Section 4 length 5.200m
10   Section 5 length 7.600m
11   Section 6 length 12.000m
12   Section 7 length 6.800m
13   Section 8 length 14.000m
14   Design waterline

15   Datum line
16   Axis of torpedo tubes
17   Keel flat (frame stations 16.0 to 57.6)
     length 41.600m
18   Navigation periscope centreline
     5.095m from after end of section 5

60

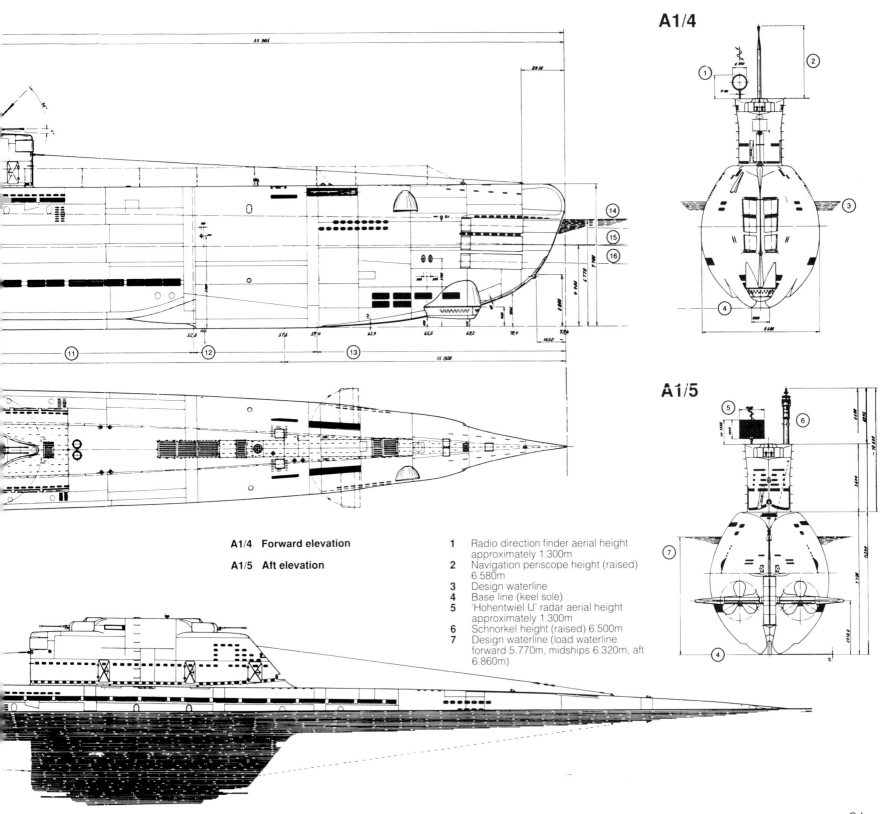

A1/4

A1/5

A1/4   Forward elevation

A1/5   Aft elevation

1   Radio direction finder aerial height
     approximately 1.300m
2   Navigation periscope height (raised)
     6.580m
3   Design waterline
4   Base line (keel sole)
5   'Hohentwiel U' radar aerial height
     approximately 1.300m
6   Schnorkel height (raised) 6.500m
7   Design waterline (load waterline
     forward 5.770m, midships 6.320m, aft
     6.860m)

61

A General arrangement and external appearance

A2/1

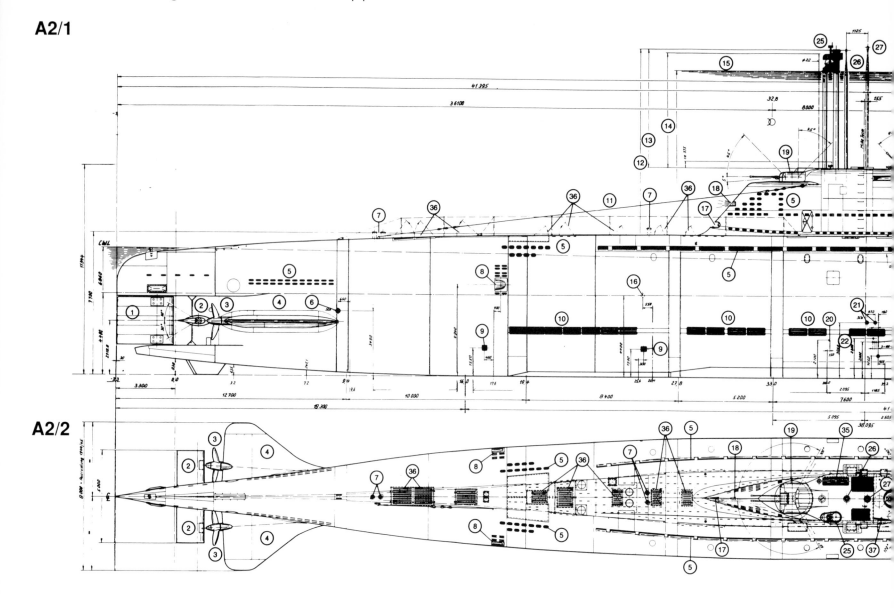

A2/2

A2 TYPE XXI TYPICAL ARRANGEMENT AS CONSTRUCTED (1944) (1/200 scale)

A2/1 Starboard elevation

A2/2 Plan of upper deck

1 Rudder
2 After hydroplanes
3 Propellers
4 Stabilisers
5 Casing flooding slots (allowing free water access to the space between pressure hull and casing when submerged)
6 Sewage outlet
7 Bollards (retractable)
8 Main engine exhaust (port and starboard)
9 Cooling water intake (port and starboard)
10 Diving tank flooding slots
11 Jumping wire and radio aerial
12 Schnorkel height from base line (keel sole) 17.700m
13 Attack periscope height approximately 5.140m
14 Schnorkel height approximately 6.100m
15 Design waterline when schnorkelling
16 Depth and trim sensor (port only)
17 Sliphook
18 Navigation light
19 Twin 20mm AA turret
20 Depth and trim sensor (starboard only)
21 Bilge pump outlet (port and starboard)
22 Mechanical log installation
23 Depth and trim sensors (starboard only)
24 Depth sensor (starboard only)
25 Schnorkel with 'Bali I' radar detector aerial
26 Attack periscope
27 Navigation periscope
28 SU 'Nibelung' sonar apparatus
29 Depth and trim sensor (port only)
30 Forward hydroplanes (retractable)
31 Underwater telephone transmitter (port and starboard)
32 GHG sound detection apparatus
33 Mechanical log installation
34 Torpedo tubes
35 'Hohentwiel U' radar transmitter/ receiver aerial
36 Deck grating (access to upper deck)
37 Radio direction finder aerial

A2/3

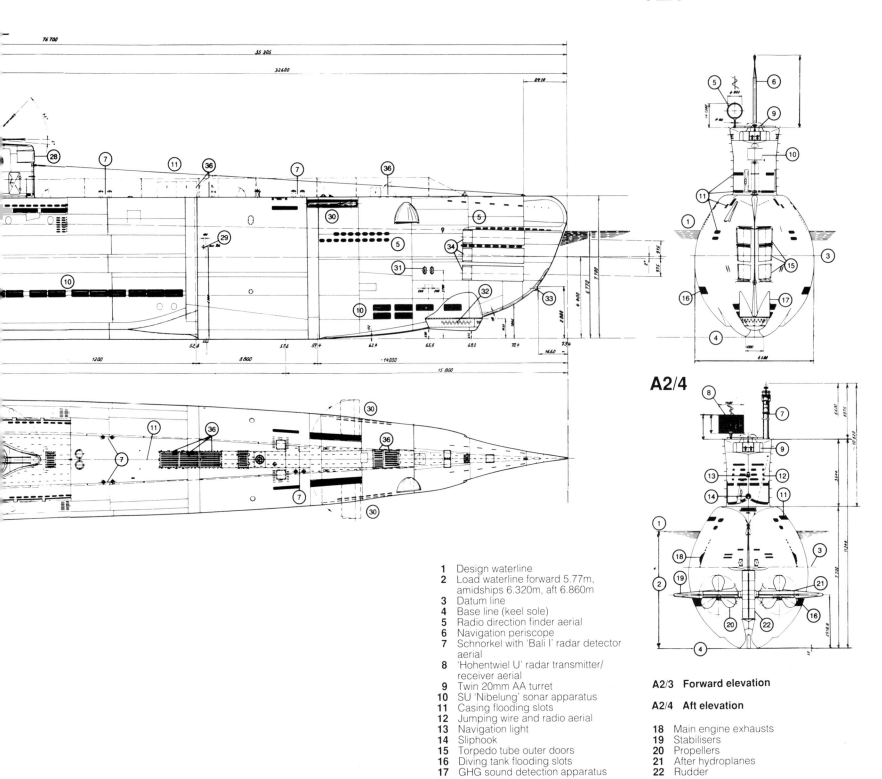

A2/3 Forward elevation

A2/4 Aft elevation

1 Design waterline
2 Load waterline forward 5.77m, amidships 6.320m, aft 6.860m
3 Datum line
4 Base line (keel sole)
5 Radio direction finder aerial
6 Navigation periscope
7 Schnorkel with 'Bali I' radar detector aerial
8 'Hohentwiel U' radar transmitter/ receiver aerial
9 Twin 20mm AA turret
10 SU 'Nibelung' sonar apparatus
11 Casing flooding slots
12 Jumping wire and radio aerial
13 Navigation light
14 Sliphook
15 Torpedo tube outer doors
16 Diving tank flooding slots
17 GHG sound detection apparatus

18 Main engine exhausts
19 Stabilisers
20 Propellers
21 After hydroplanes
22 Rudder

A General arrangement and external appearance

A2/6   **A2/7**   **A2/8**

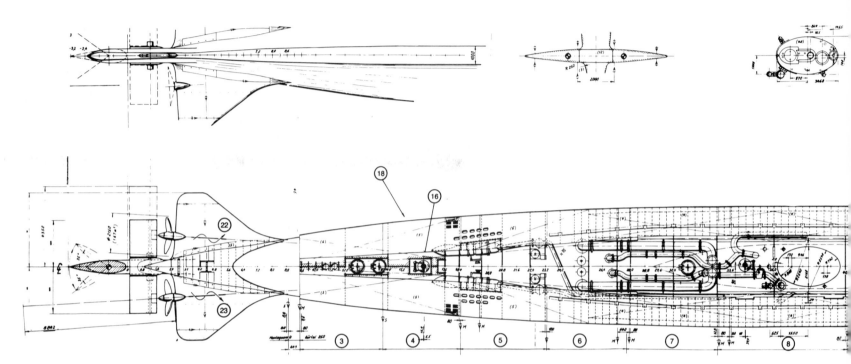

A2/5

A2/5 Plan section showing pressure hull

1   Centreline
2   Centreline of torpedo tubes
3   Casing shell 259
4   Casing shell 260
5   Casing shell 359
6   Casing shell 360
7   Casing shell 455
8   Casing shell 553
9   Casing shell 659
10 Casing shell 660/61
11 Casing shell 756/57
12 Casing shell 858
13 Casing shell 859a
14 Casing shell 861
15 Casing shell 862
16 Projected break of after hull plating
17 Projected break of bow plating at upper deck level
18 Fuel oil bunker 2a (port and starboard), frames 8.8 to 17.6/18.4; net volume 34.09cu m each
19 Diving tank 4 (port and starboard), frames 45.6 to 52.8; net volume 27.00cu m each
20 Fuel oil bunker 7a (port and starboard), frames 52.8 to 58.6; net volume 18.95cu m each
21 Watertight forecastle, frames 64.8 to 73.4; net volume 13.80 cu m
22 Port propeller (anti-clockwise rotation)
23 Starboard propeller (clockwise rotation)

A2/9

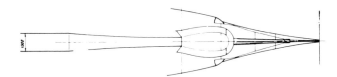

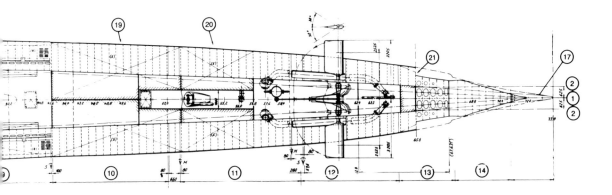

A2/6   Plan of stern from below

A2/7   Aft elevation of stabilisers

A2/8   Plan of conning tower ceiling

A2/9   Plan of bow from below

A3/1

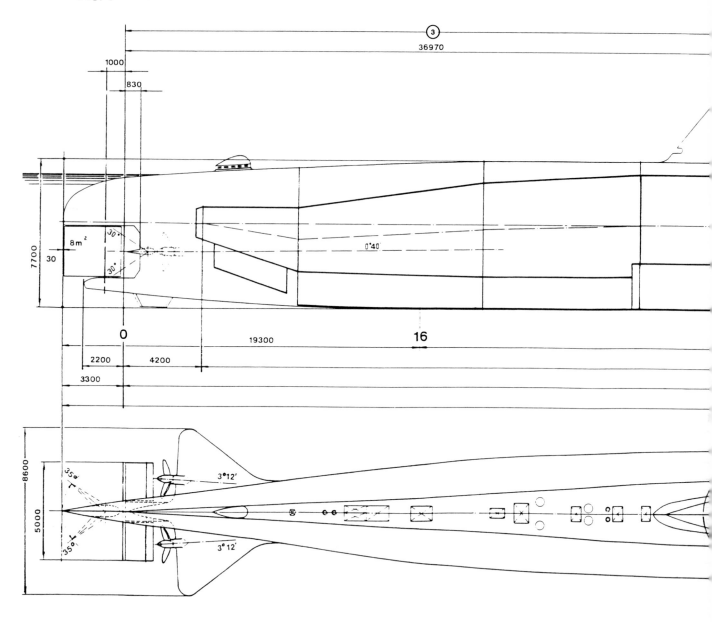

A3/2

A3	**TYPE XXI PRESSURE HULL AND CASING** (1/200 scale)
A3/1	Profile showing general arrangement and dimensions of pressure hull and casing
A3/2	Plan view of casing

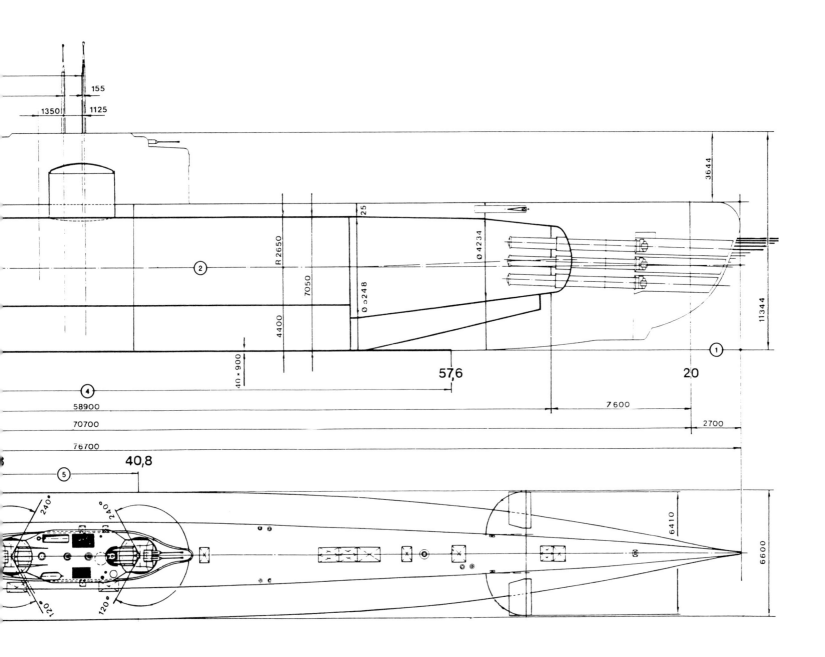

155
1350 1125
3644
25
R 2650
Ø 4234
7050
Ø 248
4400
11344
40.900
57,6
20
58900
7 600
70700
2700
76700
40,8

6410
6600

240°
240°
120°
120°

1 Base line
2 Datum line
3 Distance to conning tower transverse
centreline 37.940m
4 Keel flat 41.600m
5 Parallel sides of casing 8.00m

A3/3

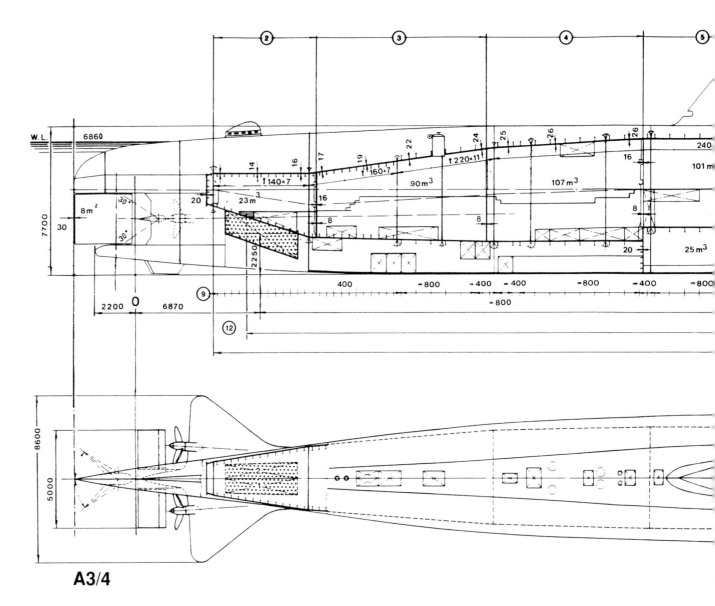

A3/4

A3/3 Profile showing pressure hull
        compartments and volumes

A3/4 Plan view of casing cut away fore
        and aft to show trimming tanks

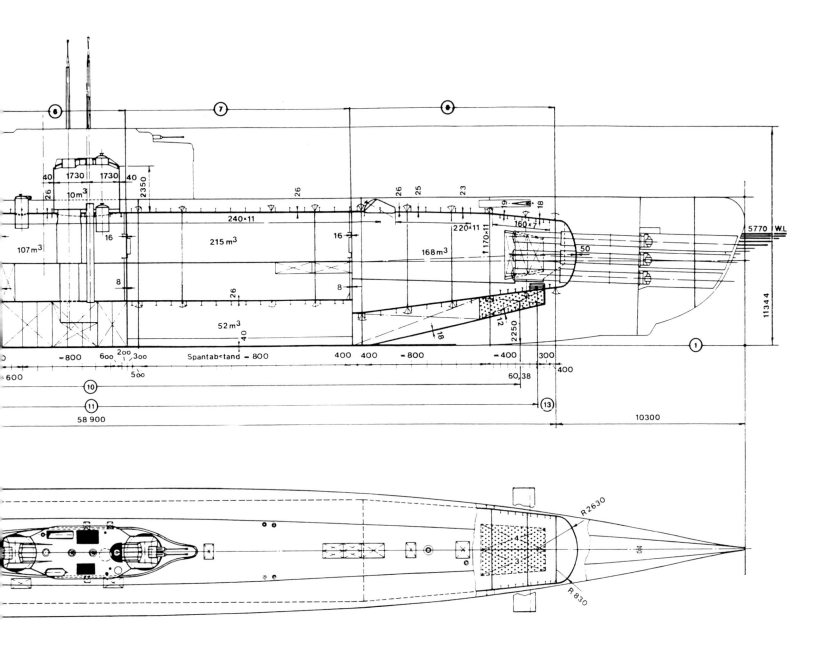

1 Base line
2 Stern compartment length 5.650m
3 Electric motor room length 9.150m
4 Diesel engine room length 8.400m
5 Crew's accommodation length 5.900m
6 Central control room length 6.700m
7 Forward accommodation length
   12.100m
8 Bow torpedo room length 11.000m
9 Frame spacing
10 Trimming tank moment 53.500m
11 Fixed ballast moment 56.000m
12 Trimming tanks 1 and 2, 3.6cu m each
13 Trimming tanks 3 and 4, 3.6cu m each

A General arrangement and external appearance

A4   U2540 (1945) RIGGED FOR DIVING   **A4/1**
      (1/200 scale)

A4/1   **Starboard elevation**

A4/2   **Plan**

A4/3   **Waterline elevation (port side)**

A4/4   **Forward elevation**

A4/5   **Aft elevation**

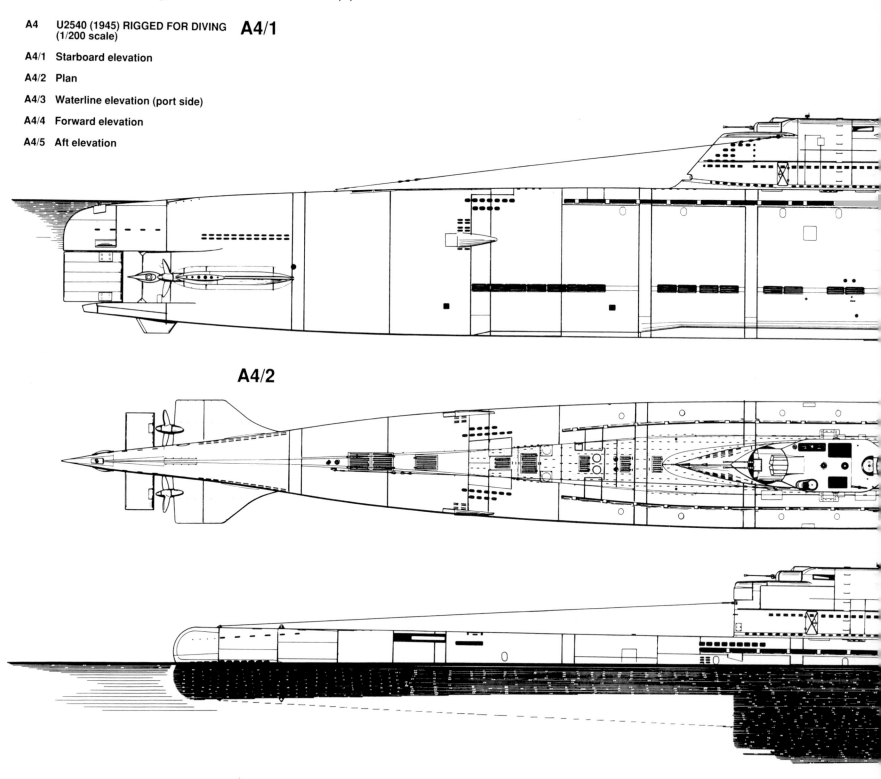

A4/2

A4/3

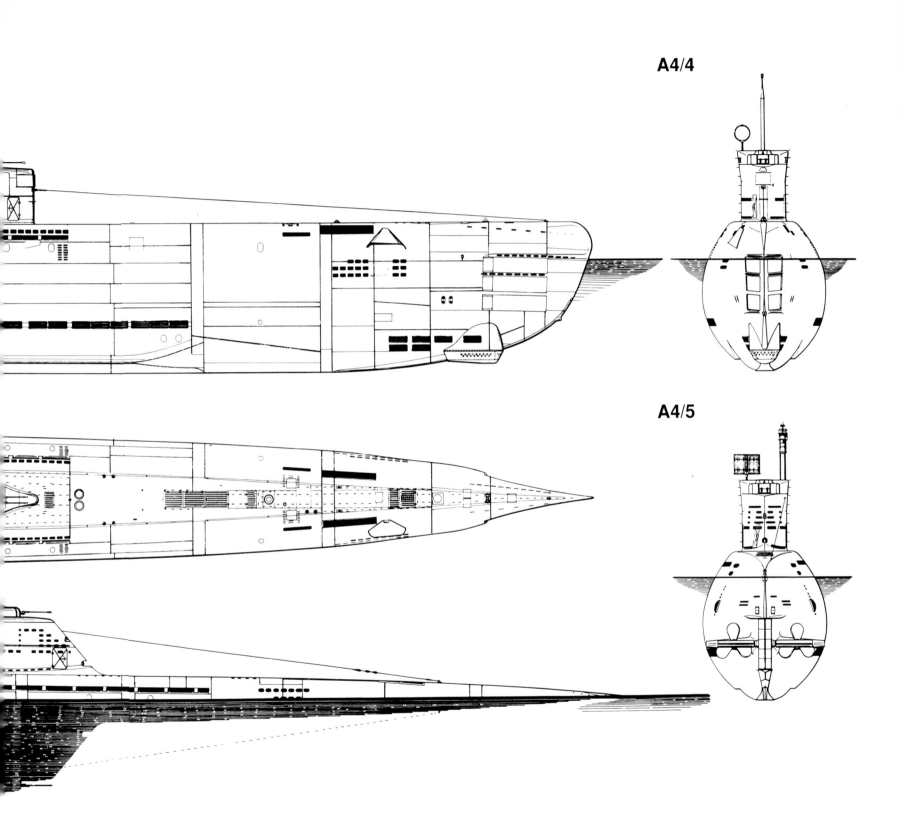

A4/4

A4/5

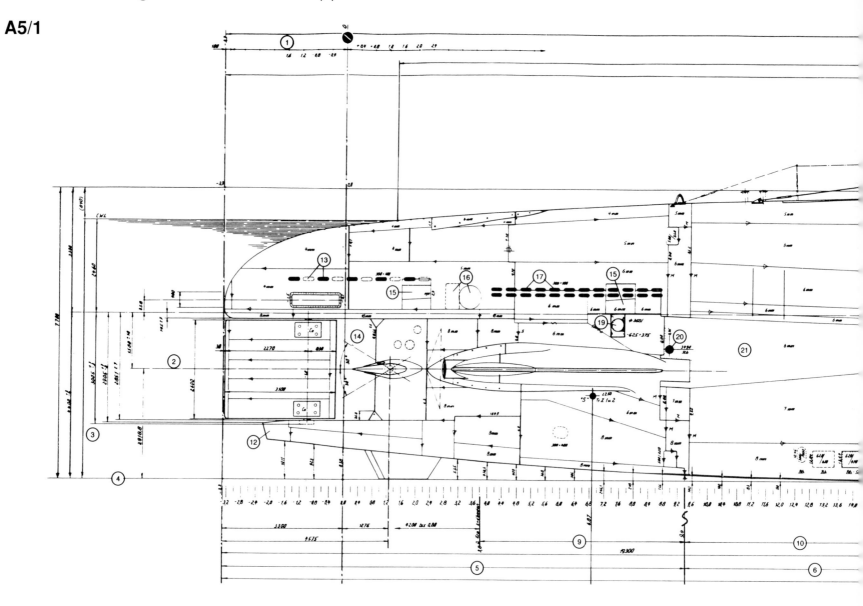

A5   TYPE XXI (1944) DETAIL VIEW OF
SECTIONS 1–3, SHOWING
PLATING AND SCANTLINGS
(1/100 scale)

A5/1   Starboard elevation

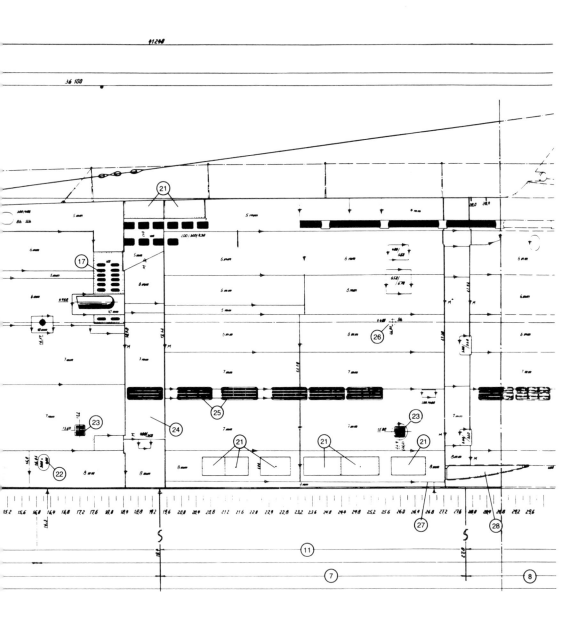

1 Frame spacing 400mm
2 Main axis
3 Loaded depth (aft) 6.860m
4 Base line (keel sole)
5 Section 1
6 Section 2
7 Section 3
8 Section 4 (part)
9 Pressure hull section 1
10 Pressure hull section 2
11 Pressure hull section 3
12 Rudder support
13 Casing flooding slots (shown dotted for port side)
14 After hydroplane radius (28 per cent only for U2513 and U3008)
15 Lifting eye
16 Assembly hatches (shown dotted for port side)
17 Casing flooding slots
18 Manhole cover (port side only)
19 Ejector for Asdic decoys
20 Sewage outlet
21 Removeable panel
22 Manhole cover
23 Cooling water intake (port and starboard)
24 Casing belt
25 Vents for diving tank 1
26 Depth and trim sensor
27 Strengthened keel plates
28 Removeable angled plates

A5/2

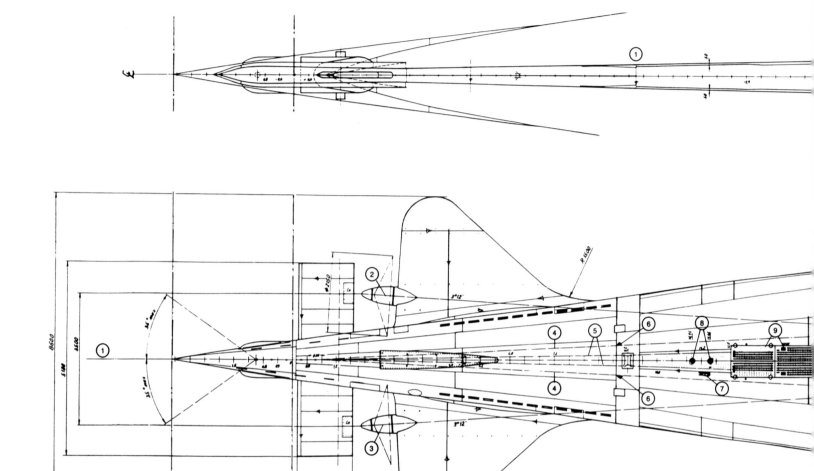

A5/3

**A5/2 Plan from below, showing keel flat
and rudder support**

1 Keelplate connection
2 Keelplate butt joint
3 Keelplate butt joint
4 Keelplate butt joint

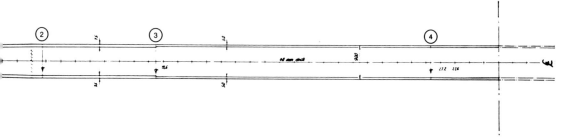

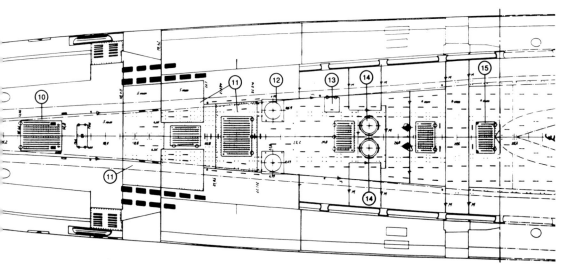

A5/3 Plan

1 Centreline
2 Three-bladed propeller, anti-clockwise
  rotation
3 Three-bladed propeller, clockwise
  rotation
4 Projected break of upper deck
5 Upper desk radius edge
6 Towing eye
7 Mounting for jumping wire/radio aerial
8 Bollard (retractable)
9 Hatch to inflatable liferaft container
10 Access hatch
11 Removeable panel
12 Compressed air inlet to diving tank 1

13 Engine oil filler
14 Compressed air inlet to diving tank 2
15 Battery hatch

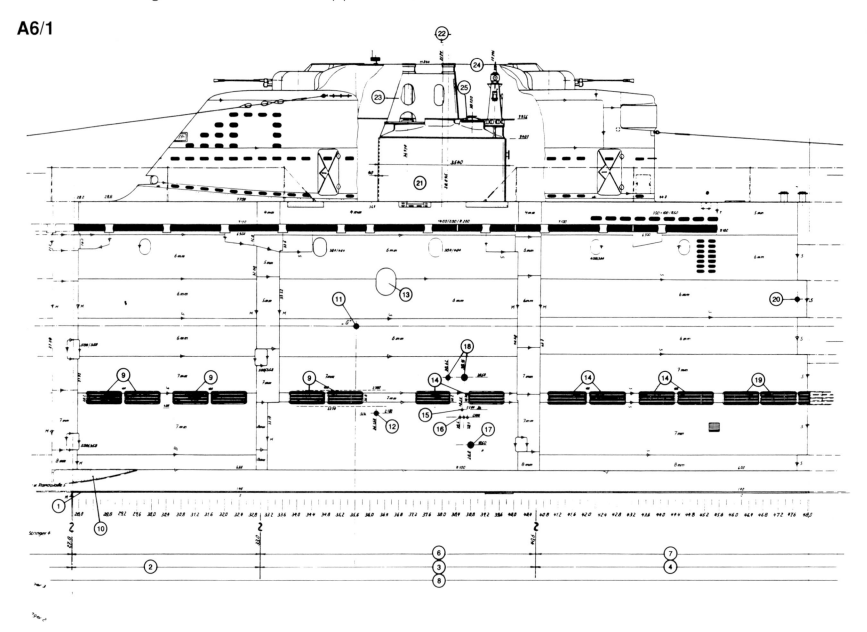

A6 TYPE XXI (1944) DETAIL VIEW OF SECTIONS 4–6, SHOWING PLATING AND SCANTLINGS (1/100 scale)

A6/1 Starboard elevation

1 Base line (keel sole)
2 Section 4 length 5.200m
3 Section 5 length 7.60m
4 Section 6 (part); total length 12.000m
5 Pressure hull section 4
6 Pressure hull section 5
7 Pressure hull section 6
8 Keel flat (frame station 16.0 to frame station 57.6) length 41.600m
9 Flooding slots for diving tank 2 (954 × 354mm)
10 Removeable angled plates
11 Centre of gravity (28.730m forward of aft trimming tank, 24.780m aft of forward trimming tank)

12 Bilge pump outlet
13 Manhole cover (port and starboard)
14 Flooding slots for diving tank 3
15 Mechanical log installation (starboard only)
16 Depth and trim sensors (starboard only)
17 Depth sensor (starboard only)
18 Bilge pump outlets
19 Flooding slots for diving tank 4
20 Sewage outlet
21 Conning tower (section 5a)
22 Centreline of conning tower
23 Periscope shelter
24 Bridge (surface steering position)
25 Conning tower hatch

A6/2

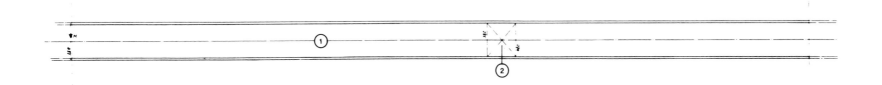

A6/3

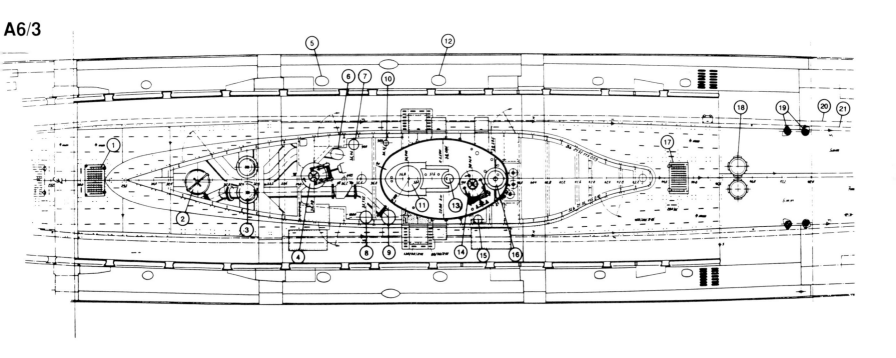

A6/2 Plan of keel flat from below, showing position of echo sounder

1 Keel sole 40mm thick
2 Position of echo sounder

A6/3 Plan

1 Battery hatch (540 × 830mm)
2 Inflatable liferaft container
3 Diesel air intake heads for surface running
4 Galley hatch
5 Manhole cover
6 Room ventilator
7 Retractable rod aerial
8 Schnorkel exhaust
9 Schnorkel air intake
10 'Hohentwiel U' radar transmitter/receiver aerial
11 Attack periscope

12 Manhole cover
13 Navigation periscope
14 Conning tower hatch
15 Radio direction finder
16 UZO surface torpedo-aiming equipment
17 Battery hatch (540 × 830mm)
18 Flooding slots for diving tank 4
19 Retractable bollards
20 Projected break of upper deck plating
21 Upper deck radius commencement point

A7/1

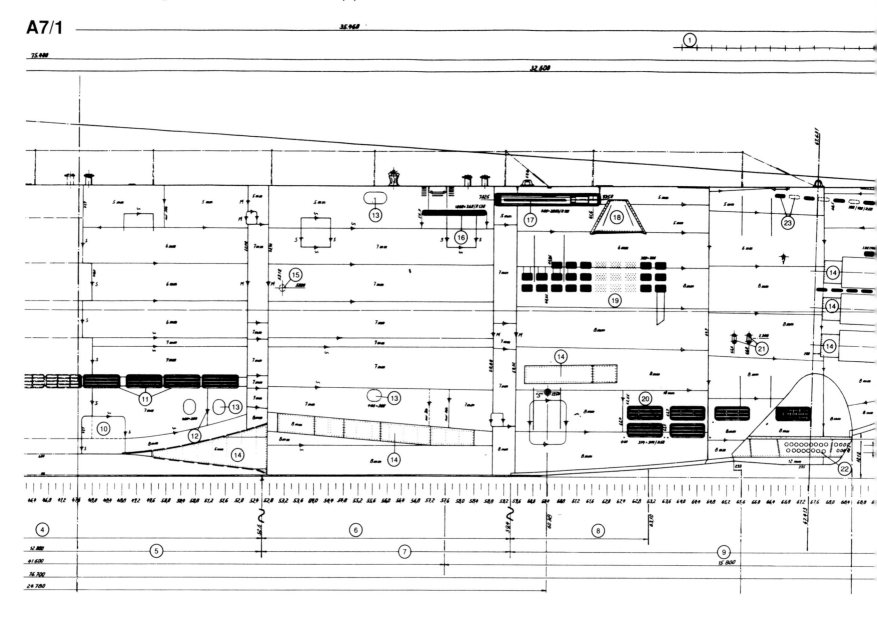

A7 TYPE XXI (1944) DETAIL VIEW OF SECTIONS 6–8, SHOWING PLATING AND SCANTLINGS (1/100 scale)

A7/1 Starboard elevation

Section A7 continued on pages 80–1

1 Frame spacing 400mm
2 Design waterline
3 Loaded depth (forward) 5.77m
4 Pressure hull section 6 (part)
5 Section 6 (part)
6 Pressure hull section 7
7 Section 7
8 Pressure hull section 8
9 Section 8
10 Plating joints on port side only shown dotted
11 Flooding slots for diving tank 4
12 Plating joint on starboard side only
13 Manhole cover
14 Removeable panel
15 Depth and trim sensor (port side only)
16 Casing flooding slot

17 Forward hydroplane
18 Hawsepipe cover (removeable)
19 Starboard side flooding slots 35mm × 25mm; port side 300mm × 200mm
20 Flooding slots for diving tank 5
21 Underwater telephone transmitter
22 GHG sound detection apparatus
23 Casing flooding slots (shown dotted for port side)
24 Torpedo tube 1 outboard tube
25 Torpedo tube 3 outboard tube
26 Torpedo tube 5 outboard tube
27 Mechanical log pressure sensor
28 Axis of outboard torpedo tubes
29 Ceiling of GHG balcony
30 Flat of stem

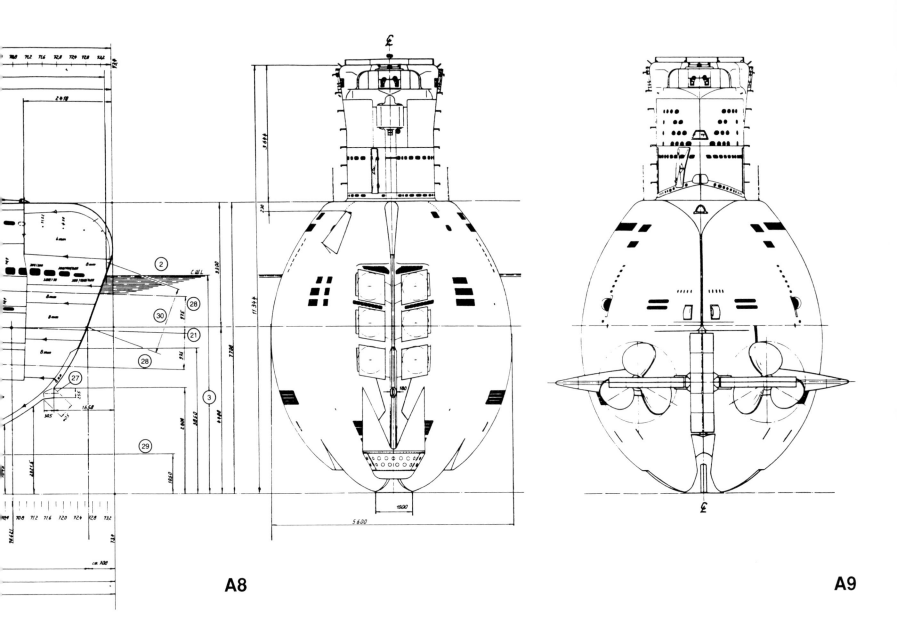

A8

A9

A8 TYPE XXI (1944) DETAILED
FORWARD ELEVATION

A9 TYPE XXI (1944) DETAILED AFT
ELEVATION

A General arrangement and external appearance

A7/2

A7/3

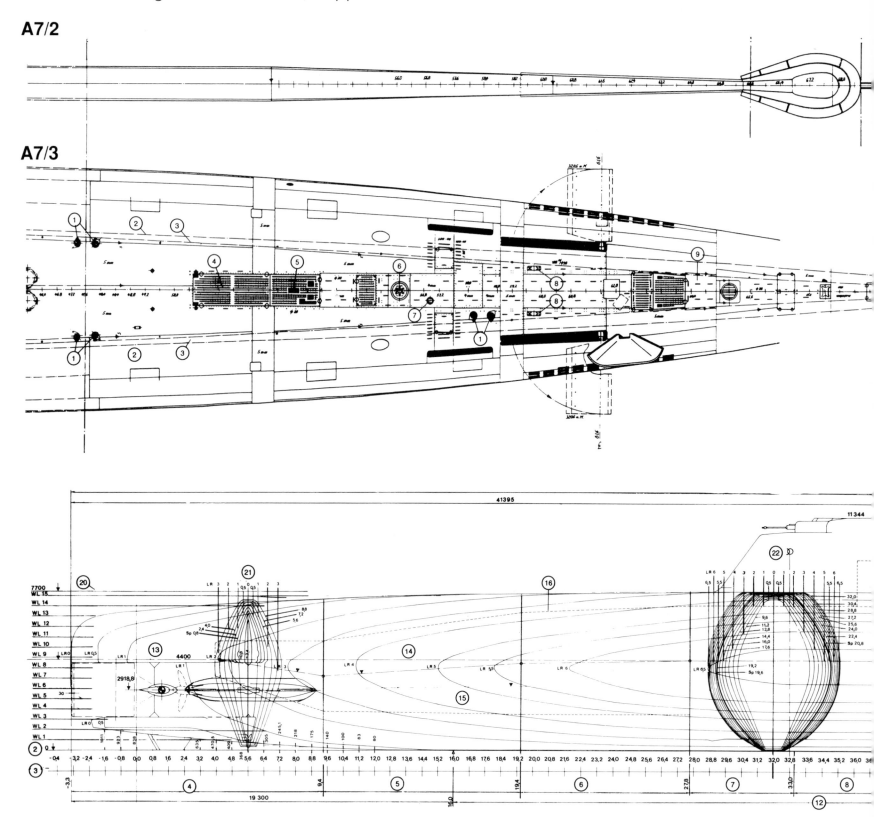

A7/2 Plan of keel and sound detection bulge from below

A7/3 Plan

1 Bollard (retractable)
2 Projected break of upper deck
3 Upper deck radius edge
4 Battery hatch
5 Torpedo loading hatch
6 Capstan (removeable)
7 Oil fuel filler cap
8 Towing eye
9 Hatch to inflatable liferaft container

1 Length overall 76.700m
2 Base line
3 Frame stations
4 Section 1 length 12.700m
5 Section 2 length 10.000m
6 Section 3 length 8.400m
7 Section 4 length 5.200m
8 Section 5 length 7.600m
9 Section 6 length 12.000m
10 Section 7 length 6.800m
11 Section 8 length 14.000m
12 Keel flat (frame stations 16.0 to 57.6) length 41.600m
13 Datum line
14 Pressure hull axis
15 Axis of propeller shafts
16 Profile of pressure hull
17 Conning tower centreline
18 Centreline of navigation periscope
19 Centreline of torpedo tubes
20 Upper deck
21 Body lines 2.4 to 8.8
22 Body lines 9.6 to 32.0
23 Body lines 32.8 to 65.6
24 Body lines 59.4 to 73.4

B1   TYPE XXI (1944) HULL LINES (1/200 scale)

B1/1   Waterlines, centreline to 6.5m; also showing body lines 2.4 to 8.8, 9.6 to 32.0. 32.8 to 65.6 and 59.4 to 73.4

B1/1

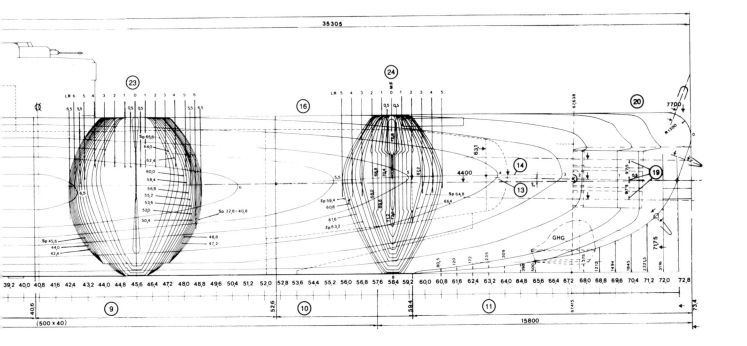

B2

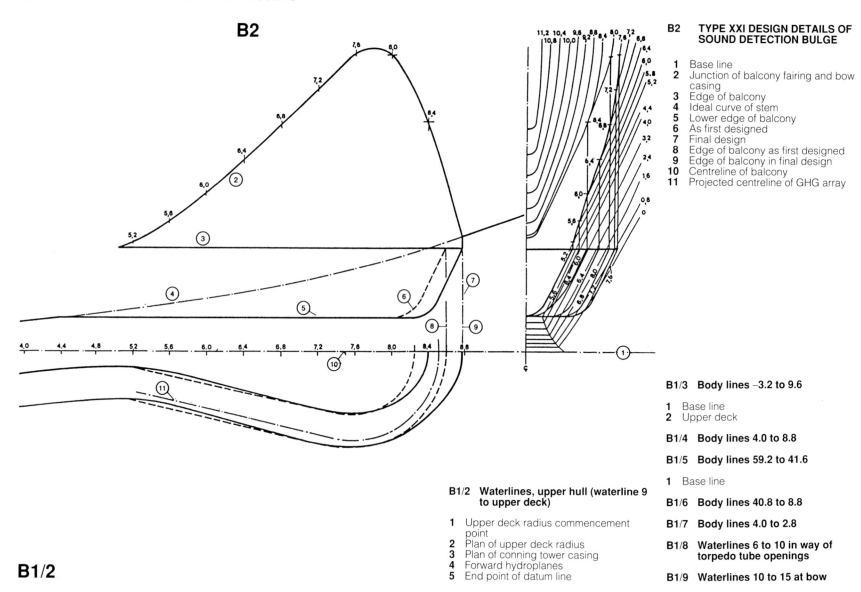

B2 TYPE XXI DESIGN DETAILS OF SOUND DETECTION BULGE

1 Base line
2 Junction of balcony fairing and bow casing
3 Edge of balcony
4 Ideal curve of stem
5 Lower edge of balcony
6 As first designed
7 Final design
8 Edge of balcony as first designed
9 Edge of balcony in final design
10 Centreline of balcony
11 Projected centreline of GHG array

B1/3 Body lines −3.2 to 9.6

1 Base line
2 Upper deck

B1/4 Body lines 4.0 to 8.8

B1/5 Body lines 59.2 to 41.6

1 Base line

B1/6 Body lines 40.8 to 8.8

B1/7 Body lines 4.0 to 2.8

B1/8 Waterlines 6 to 10 in way of torpedo tube openings

B1/9 Waterlines 10 to 15 at bow

B1/2 Waterlines, upper hull (waterline 9 to upper deck)

1 Upper deck radius commencement point
2 Plan of upper deck radius
3 Plan of conning tower casing
4 Forward hydroplanes
5 End point of datum line

B1/2

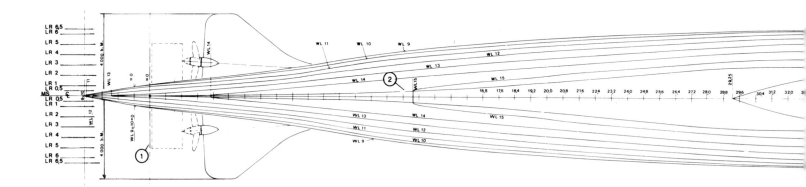

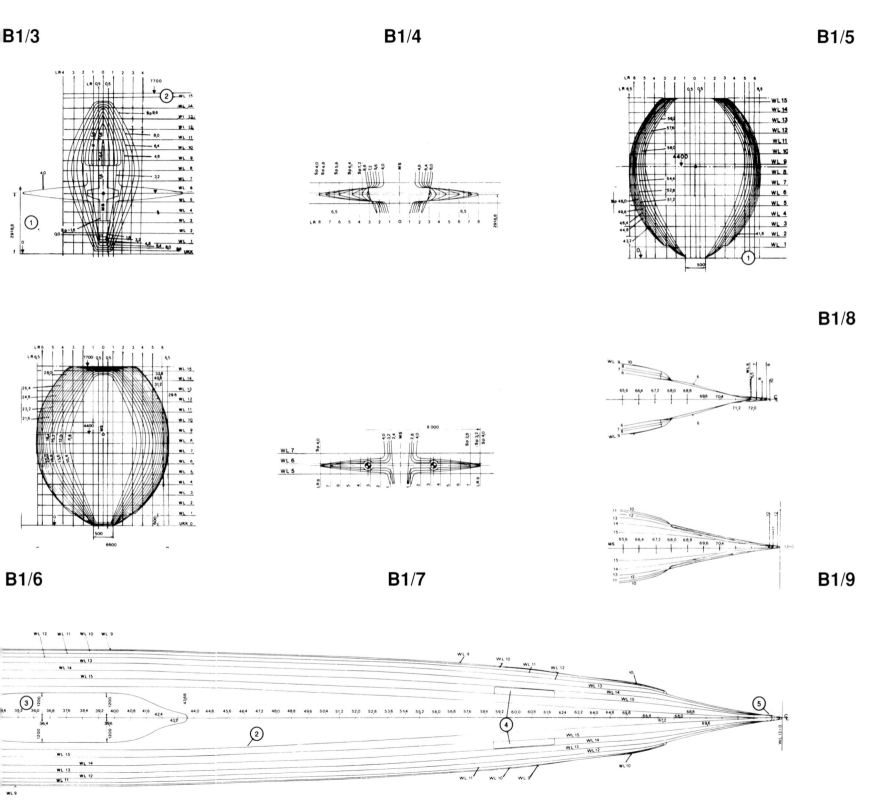

B1/3

B1/4

B1/5

B1/8

B1/6

B1/7

B1/9

Section B1 continued on pages 84–5

B Lines and constructional details

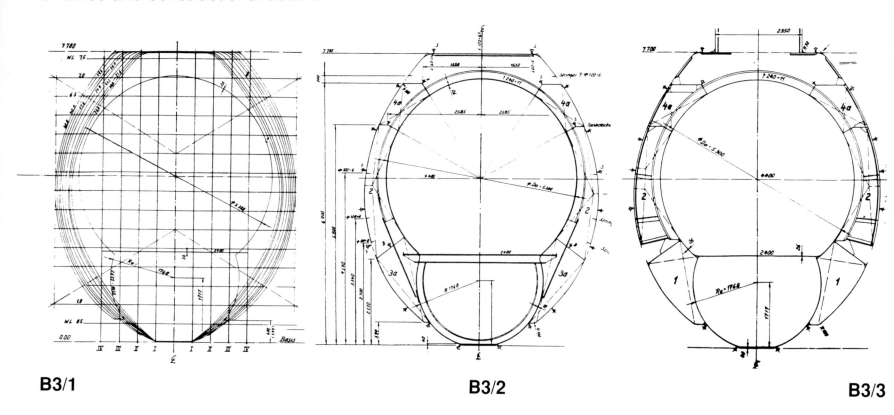

B3/1

B3/2

B3/3

B1/11

B1/10 Waterlines, lower hull (keel flat to waterline 9)

1   Plan of pressure hull
2   Propeller shaft axis
3   Keel flat
4   Centreline of torpedo tubes

B1/11 Waterlines 1 to 3 at stern in way of rudder support

B1/12 Waterlines 0 to 5 at bow, showing hull shape beneath sound detection bulge

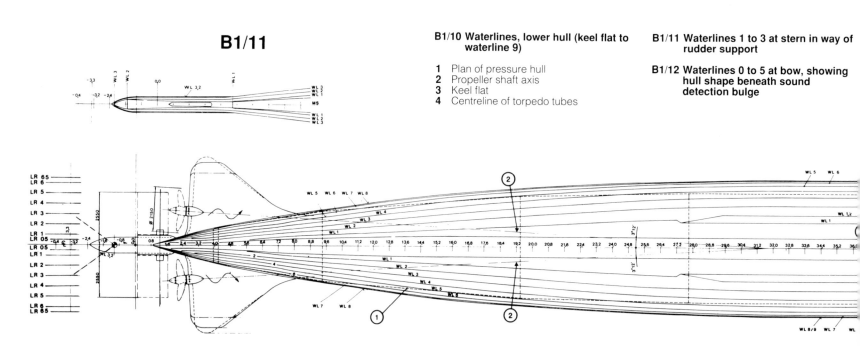

B1/10

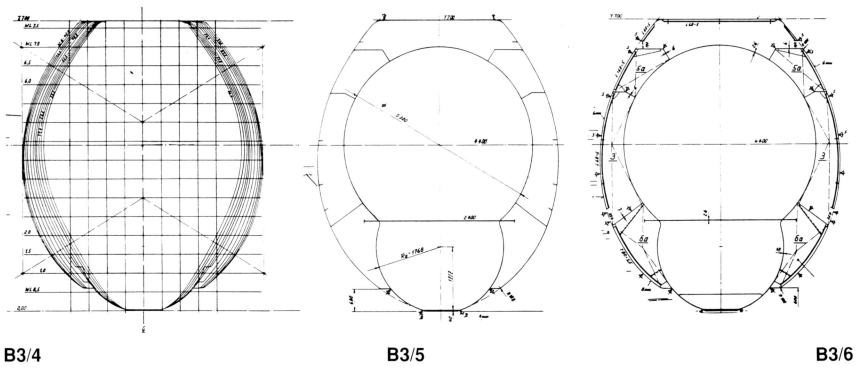

B3/4　　　　　　　　　　　　**B3/5**　　　　　　　　　　　　**B3/6**

B3 TYPE XXI (1944) FRAME DESIGN
DETAILS (MIDSHIPS FRAMES)
(1/100 scale)

B3/1 Frame station lines 20.0 to 40.8
showing internal dimensions

B3/2 Frame 28.0 (28.4 to 32.4 identical)
showing dimensions, construction
details and compartments

B3/3 Frame 35.2 showing dimensions,
construction details and
compartments

B3/4 Frame station lines 32.8 to 56.0

B3/5 Frames 32.8 to 40.8, showing
internal dimensions

B3/6 Frames 32.8 to 41.2, showing
dimensions, construction details
and compartments

B1/12

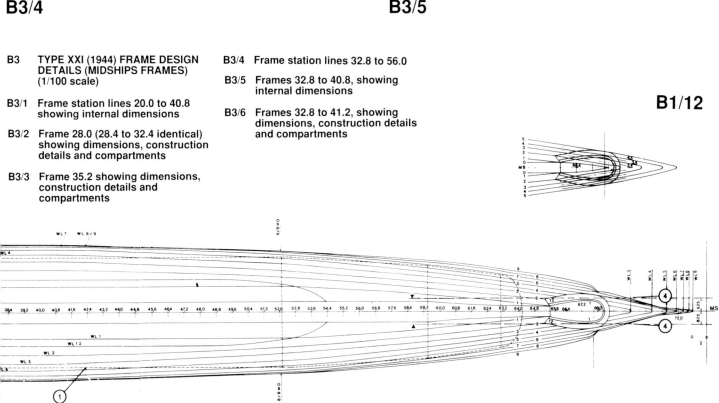

C Internal arrangement

C1/1

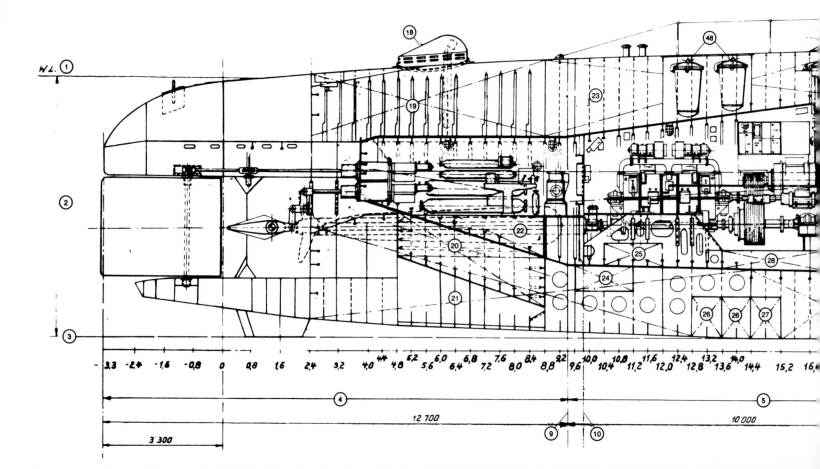

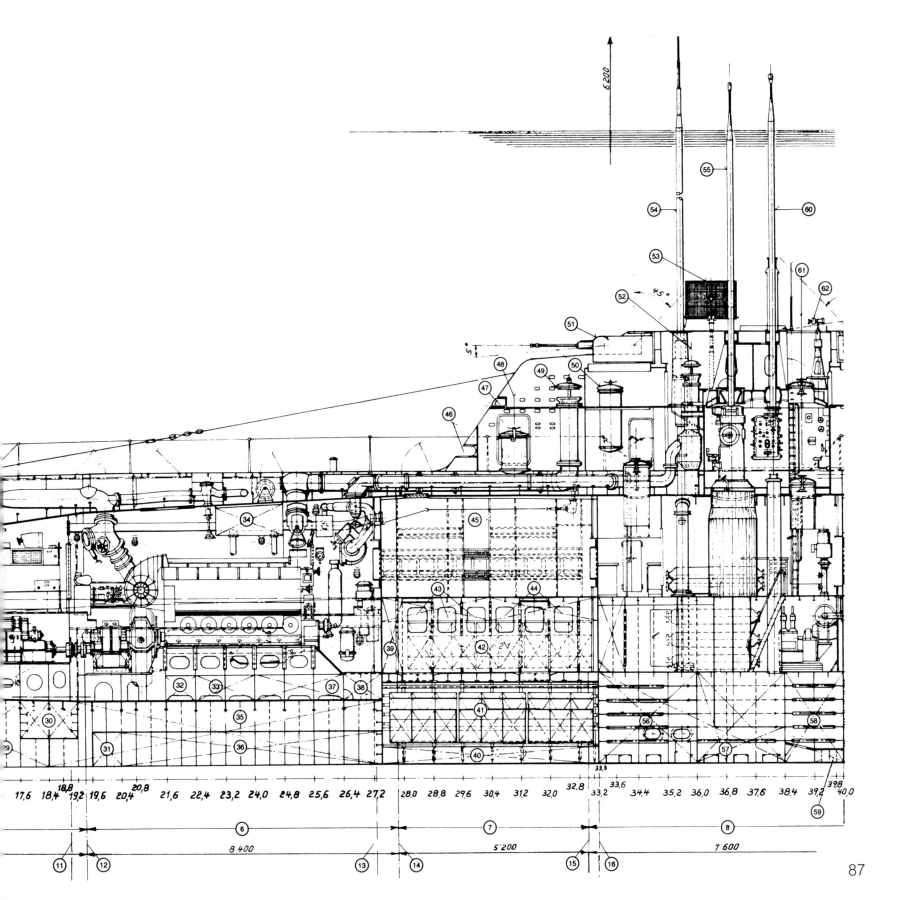

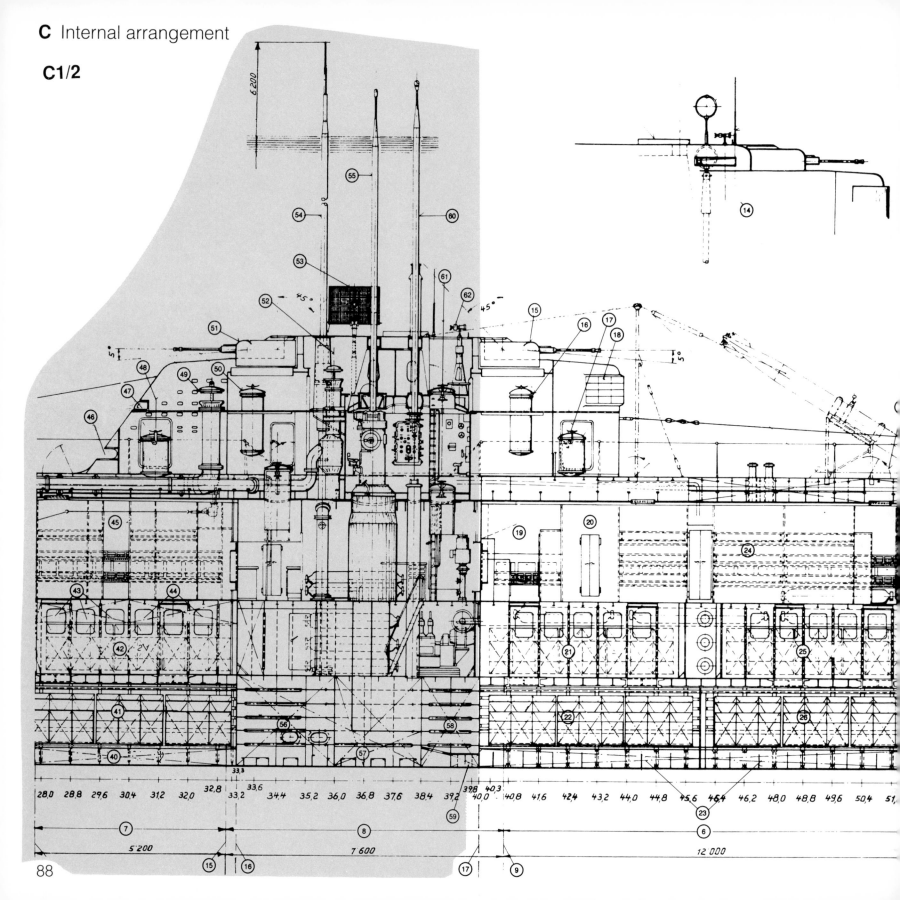

C1/2 Internal profile, sections 4 to 8

1 Upper deck level
2 Load waterline
3 Datum line
4 Loaded depth (forward) 5.770m
5 Base line (keel sole)
6 Section 6 (forward accommodation) c150t
7 Section 7 (bow torpedo room) c90t
8 Section 8 (torpedo tubes) c125t
9 Butt joint 40.6
10 Bulkhead 52.1
11 Butt joint 52.6
12 Butt joint 59.4
13 Butt joint 63.1
14 Detail showing radio direction finder aerial raised and retracted
15 Flat turret
16 Ready use ammunition container
17 Inflatable liferaft container
18 SU apparatus
19 Commander's quarters
20 Listening room
21 Battery compartment 2.2
22 Battery compartment 1.2
23 Ballast compartment 4 (sealed)
24 Forward crew accommodation
25 Battery compartment 2.3
26 Battery compartment 1.3
27 Battery hatch
28 Torpedo hatch
29 Fuel oil bunker 7a
30 Containers for torpedo warhead pistols
31 Torpedo compensating tank (port and starboard)
32 Trimming tanks 3 and 4
33 Torpedo firing controller's seat
34 Forward hydroplane
35 Inflatable liferaft container
36 Ballast compartment 6 (sealed)
37 Ballast compartment 7
38 Ballast compartment 8 (sealed)
39 Diving tank 5
40 Free flooding space
41 Watertight forecastle (13.8cu m)
42 GHG sound-detection apparatus
43 High pressure water section of ballast compartment

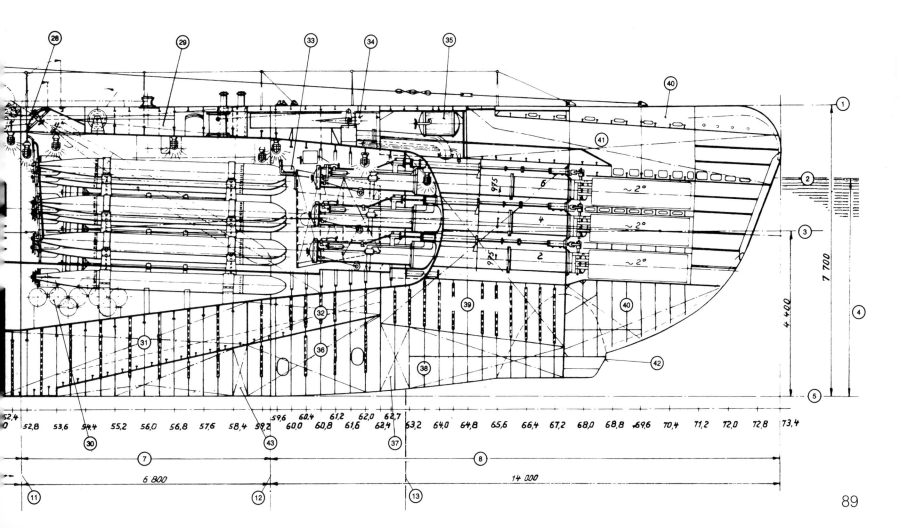

89

C Internal arrangement

C1/3 Plan at main deck level, sections 1 to 5

1 Oil-tight bulkhead 8.8
2 Oil-tight bulkhead 18.4
3 Watertight bulkhead 25.6
4 Bulkhead 27.4
5 Watertight bulkhead 36.0
6 Rudder (c8sq m)

24 Silent running V-belt transmission
25 Silent running motor
26 Electric compass transformer 2 (left); AC transformer 2 (right)
27 Main engine control position
28 Fuel oil bunker 2 (port and starboard)
29 Diving tank 1 (starboard)
30 Starter oil pump
31 Diesel engine transmission

55 Potato locker (cool room) filling hatch
56 Auxiliary switchboard 2
57 Schnorkel
58 Attack periscope well
59 Oxygen cylinders
60 High pressure/low pressure tank blowing console
61 Depth control position
62 Radio direction finder

63 Steering position
64 Master gyro compass
65 Retractable rod aerial
66 'Hohentwiel U' radar transmitter/ receiver aerial
67 Navigator's desk
68 High pressure air cylinder group 5
69 High pressure oil tanks
70 High pressure oil pumps

C1/3

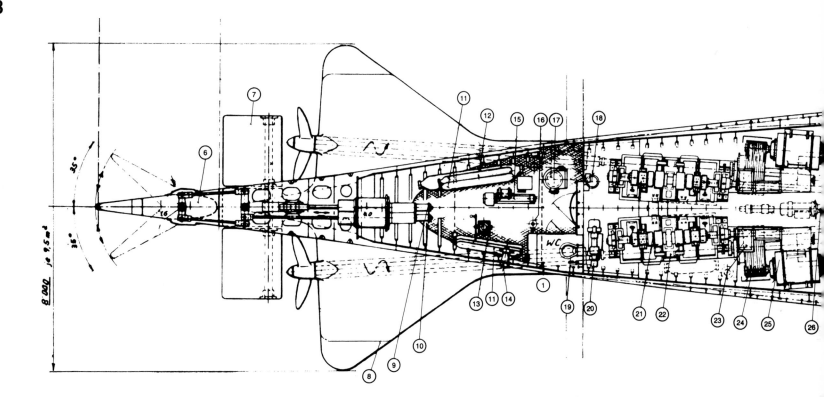

7 After hydroplanes (c3sq m each)
8 Shape of stabilisers from U2540
9 Hydroplane drive
10 Rudder drive
11 Oxygen cylinders
12 Compressed air cylinder group 1
13 Emergency rudder controls
14 'Bold' asdic decoy ejector
15 Lathe
16 Electric drill
17 Bilge pump 1
18 Cooling water pump
19 After WC with sewage tank
20 Electric compass transformer 1 (above); AC transformer 1 (below)
21 Fan for electric motors
22 Main electric motor Type 2 GU 365/30 'Hertha' (1510/1840kw; 1570/1680rpm; 330/502V; 4500/5500A); auxiliary switchboard 1 and silent running control position (right)
23 (Port side) silent running control position (left) and electric current switchboard

32 Junkers 4 FK 115 air compressor
33 MAN diesel engine
34 Vulkan clutch
35 Drinking water condenser
36 Diving tank 1 (port)
37 Compressors
38 Air purifying installations
39 Diesel air duct
40 Engine oil cooler
41 Condensers
42 Auxiliary motors
43 Engine oil replacement pump
44 Engine oil filter unit
45 Crew accommodation (note: sp = locker, numbers show tiers of berths)
46 Diving tank 2 (port)
47 Diving tank 2 (starboard)
48 Watertight hatches
49 Galley
50 Electric cooker
51 Provision store
52 Washbasin
53 Freezer
54 Central control room

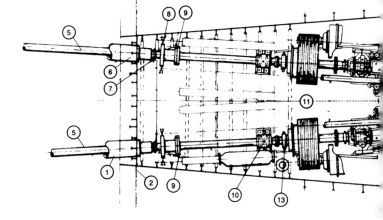

C1/4

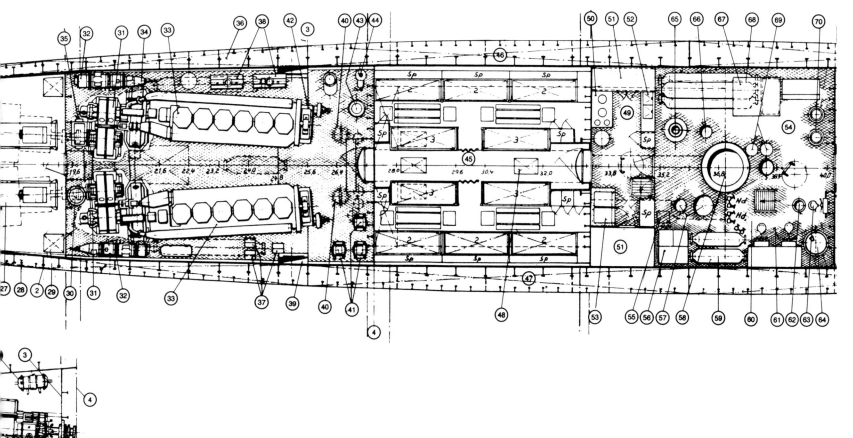

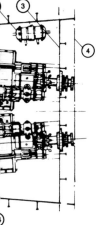

**C1/4   Plan of electric motor room
(section 2) below main deck level**

1   Butt joint 9.4
2   Bulkhead 9.85
3   Bulkhead 19.2
4   Butt joint 19.4
5   Propeller shaft
6   Propeller shaft bearings
7   Propeller shaft oil seals
8   Shaft brake
9   Shaft clutch flange
10 Shaft bearings
11 Walkway between electric motors
12 Gear oil cooler
13 Silent running motor clutch
14 Electric motor transmission

C1/5

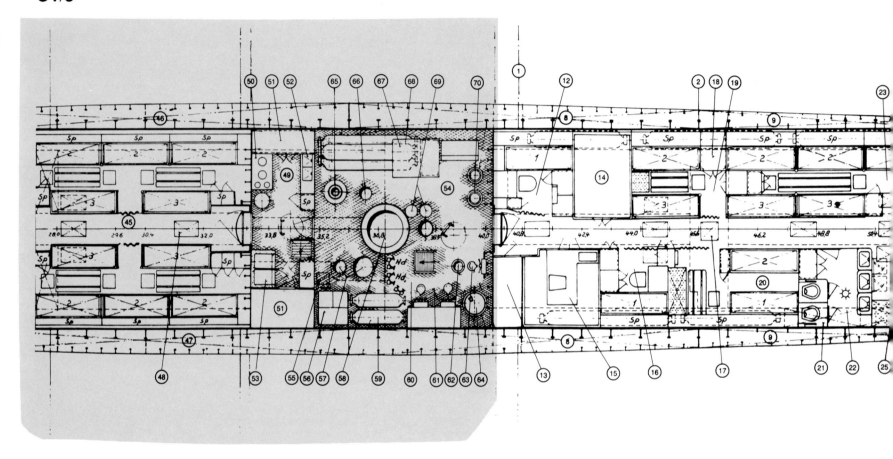

C1/5 Plan at main deck level, sections 4 to 8

1 Butt joint 40.6
2 Watertight bulkhead 45.6
3 Bulkhead 52.1
4 Butt joint 52.6
5 Oil-tight bulkhead 52.8
6 Oil-tight bulkhead 58.8
7 Butt joint 49.4
8 Diving tank 3 (port and starboard)
9 Diving tank 4 (port and starboard)
10 Fuel oil bunker 7a (port and starboard)
11 Diving tank 5
12 Commander's quarters
13 Sickbay
14 Listening room
15 Radio room
16 Chief engineer's quarters
17 Provision store hatch (battery hatches forward and aft)
18 Battery circuit breaker 1
19 Senior ratings' quarters
20 Officers' quarters

21 Two WCs
22 Wash room with drying locker for waterproof clothing
23 Petty officers' quarters
24 Chart locker
25 Senior ratings' quarters
26 Battery circuit breaker 2
27 Torpedo ejection air distributor
28 Reload torpedos
29 Torpedo compensating tanks for tubes 1, 3 and 5 (as numbered)
30 Torpedo compensating tanks for tubes 2, 4 and 6 (as numbered)
31 Torpedo ejection compressed air cylinders
32 LUT adjuster device
33 Outer torpedo tubes 2, 4 and 6
34 Outer torpedo tubes 1, 3 and 5
35 Torpedo tube outer doors
36 Casing doors for torpedos
Sp Locker

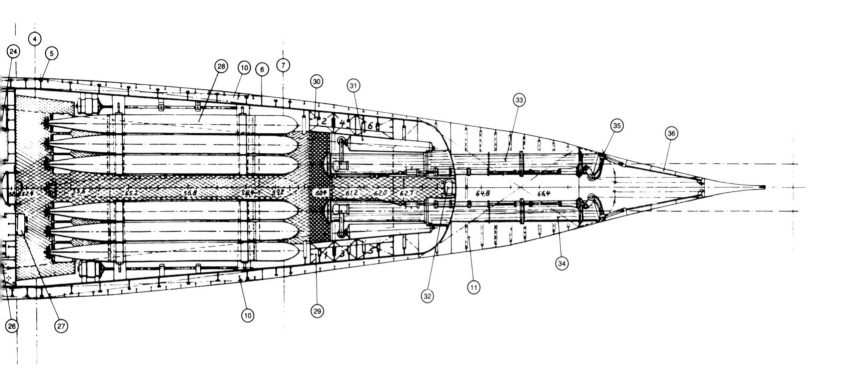

C Internal arrangement

C2 **TYPE XXI (1944) SECTIONS SHOWING INTERNAL ARRANGEMENT**
(1/100 scale)

C2/1

C2/2

C2/3

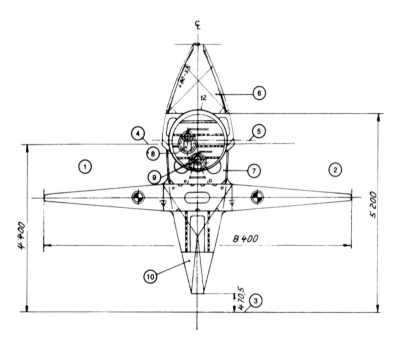

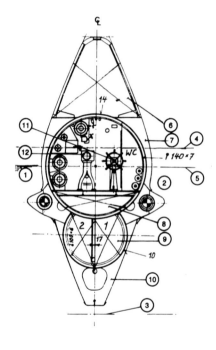

C2/1 Frame 4.0 looking aft

1 Starboard
2 Port
3 Base line (keel sole)
4 Datum line
5 Pressure hull axis
6 Watertight stern compartment
7 Free-flooding space
8 Rudder drive
9 After hydroplane drive
10 Fuel oil bunker 1a, frames 2.4 to 14.4
(30.68cu m)

C2/2 Frame 7.6 looking forward, showing the emergency steering position

1 Port
2 Starboard
3 Base line (keel sole)
4 Datum line
5 Pressure hull axis
6 Watertight stern compartment, frames 2.4 to 8.8 (15.52cu m)
7 Free-flooding space
8 Reserve lubricating oil tank, frames 6.4 to 8.8 (3.17cu m)
9 Trimming tanks 1 and 2, frames 4.8 to 8.8 93.60cu m each)
10 Fuel oil bunker 1a, frames 2.4 to 14.4 (30.68cu m)
11 Emergency steering position
12 Lathe

C2/3 Frame 8.0 looking forward, looking on bulkhead 9.85

3 Base line (keel sole)
4 Datum line
5 Pressure hull axis
6 Watertight stern compartment
7 Electric drill
8 Bilge pump 1

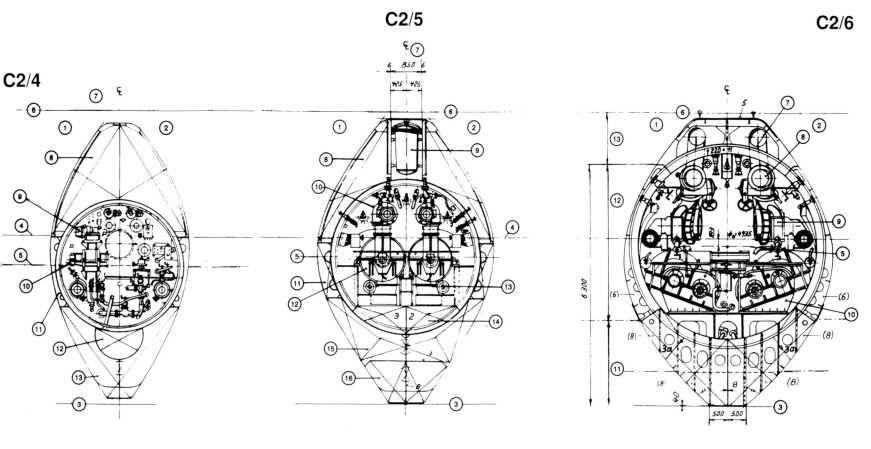

C2/4

C2/5

C2/6

C2/4 Frame 10.0 looking aft, looking on bulkhead 9.85

1 Starboard
2 Port
3 Base line (keel sole)
4 Datum
5 Pressure hull axis
6 Upper deck level
7 Designed break of hull plating
8 Fuel oil bunker 2a (port and starboard), frames 8.8 to 18.4 (each 34.09 cu m)
9 Electric ompass transformer 1
10 AC transformer 1
11 Free-flooding space
12 Bilge water tank, frames 9.6 to 11.2 (1.22cu m)
13 Fuel oil bunker 1a, frames 2.4 to 14.4 (30.68cu m)

C2/5 Frame 14.0 looking aft

1 Starboard
2 Port
3 Base line (keel sole)
4 Datum line
5 Pressure hull axis
6 Upper deck level
7 Space for inflatable liferaft containers, frames 12.0 to 14.4
8 Fuel oil bunker 2a
9 Inflatable liferaft container
10 Fan for electric motors
11 Free-flooding space
12 Main electric motor Type 2 GU 365/30 'Hertha'
13 Propeller shaft
14 Reserve lubricating oil tanks, frames 13.2 to 16.4 (1.86cu m each)
15 Fuel oil bunker 1a

16 Adjustable ballast tank (2.04cu m)

C2/6 Auxiliary bulkhead 19.6, looking forward

1 Port
2 Starboard
3 Base line (keel sole)
4 Datum line
5 Pressure hull axis
6 Upper deck level
7 Engine exhaust trunking
8 Engine exhaust valve
9 Engine exhaust fan
10 Diesel engine transmission
11 Fuel oil bunker 3a (port and starboard), frames 18.4 to 33.3 (33.5cu m each)
12 Diving tank 1 (port and starboard), frames 18.4 to 25.6 (17.10cu m each)

13 Free-flooding space

C2/7

C2/8

C2/9

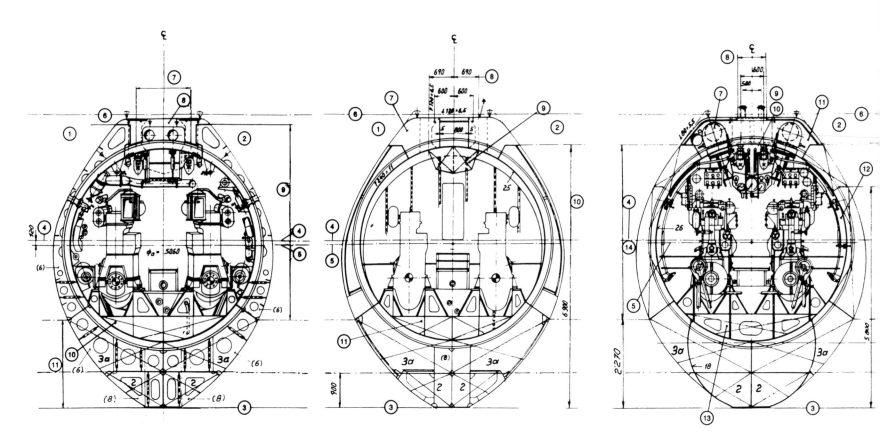

C2/7 Support bulkhead 60mm aft of frame 22.4, looking forward

1   Port
2   Starboard
3   Base line (keel sole)
4   Datum line
5   Pressure hull axis
6   Upper deck level
7   Vent valves for diving tank 1
8   Free-flooding space
9   Diving tank 1 (port and starboard)
10 Fuel oil drain tank, frames 21.6 to 22.4 (11.32cu m)
11 Sub-dividing bulkheads

C2/8 Frame 23.2 looking forward

1   Port
2   Starboard
3   Base line (keel sole)
4   Datum line
5   Pressure hull axis
6   Upper deck level
7   Free-flooding space
8   Vent valves for diving tank 1 (at frame station 22. 59)
9   High level fuel oil reservoir
10 Diving tank 1 (port and starboard), frames 18.4 to 25.6 (17.10cu m each)
11 Lubricating oil drain tanks (port and starboard), frames 22.4 to 24.0 (1.33cu m each)

C2/9 Frame 24.8, looking aft to frame 26.4

1   Starboard
2   Port
3   Base line (keel sole)
4   Datum line
5   Pressure hull axis
6   Upper deck level
7   Diesel exhaust trunking with lower valve
8   Hatches (830 × 540mm)
9   Vent valves for diving tank 2 (at frame station 25.2)
10 Diesel engine main controls
11 Free-flooding space
12 Diesel air intake duct
13 Reserve lubricating oil tank 4, frames 24.0 to 26.4 (3.92cu m)

14 Diving tank 1 (port and starboard), frames 18.4 to 25.6 17.10 cu m)

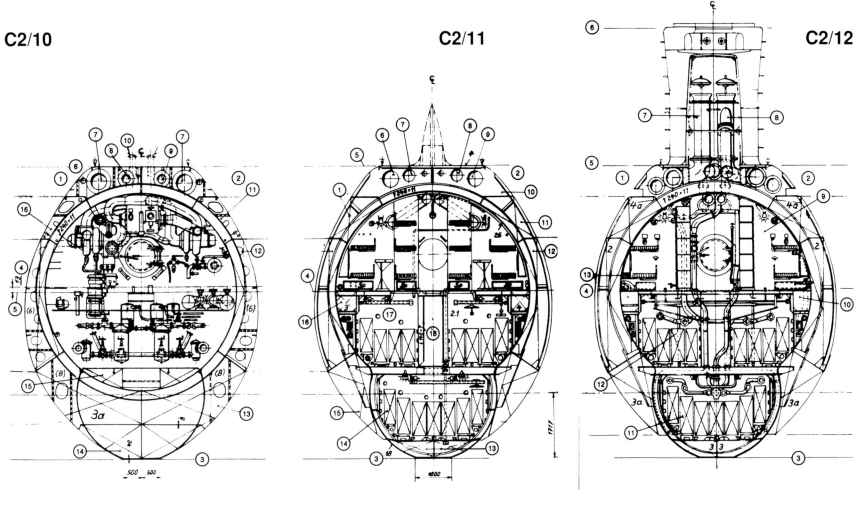

C2/10

C2/11

C2/12

C2/10 Frame 26.4 looking forward, looking on bulkhead 27.4 and auxiliary bulkhead 27.2

1 Port
2 Starboard
3 Base line (keel sole)
4 Datum line
5 Pressure hull axis
6 Upper deck level
7 Diesel air intake trunking
8 Room ventilation exhaust trunking
9 Room ventilation air intake trunking
10 Retractable bollards
11 Fuel oil bunker 4a (port and starboard), frames 25.6 to 36.0 (9.49cu m each)
12 Diving tank 2 (port and starboard), frames 25.6 to 36.0 (22.80cu m each)
13 Fuel oil bunker 3a (port and starboard), frames 18.4 to 33.3 (33.50 cu m each)
14 Ballast compartment 2 (sealed)
15 Dirty lubricating oil tank, frames 26.4 to 27.4 (1.07cu m)
16 Supporting bulkhead 27.2

C2/11 Frame 28.8 looking aft, showing crew's quarters

1 Starboard
2 Port
3 Base line (keel sole)
4 Datum line and pressure hull axis
5 Upper deck level
6 Diesel air intake trunking
7 Room ventilation exhaust trunking
8 Room ventilation intake trunking
9 Diesel air intake trunking
10 Free-flooding space
11 Fuel oil bunker 4a (port and starboard), frames 25.6 to 36.0 (9.49cu m each)
12 Diving tank 2 (port and starboard), frames 25.6 to 36.0 (22.80cu m each)
13 Ballast compartment 3 (sealed)
14 Battery compartment 1.1
15 Fuel oil bunker 4a (port and starboard), frames 18.4 to 33.3 (33.50cu m each)
16 Drinking water tanks 3 (starboard) and 4 (port)
17 Battery compartment 2.1
18 Battery access companionway

C2/12 Frame 32.0 looking forward, looking on auxiliary bulkhead 32.8

1 Port
2 Starboard
3 Base line (keel sole)
4 Datum line and pressure hull axis
5 Upper deck level
6 Roof of conning tower casing
7 Diesel air intakes (port and starboard)
8 Room ventilation air intake connection (starboard side only); schnorkel air intake trunking below and forward
9 Crew accommodation
10 Provision store (port and starboard)
11 Battery compartment 1.1
12 Battery compartment 2.1
13 Cable trough

C2/13

C2/14

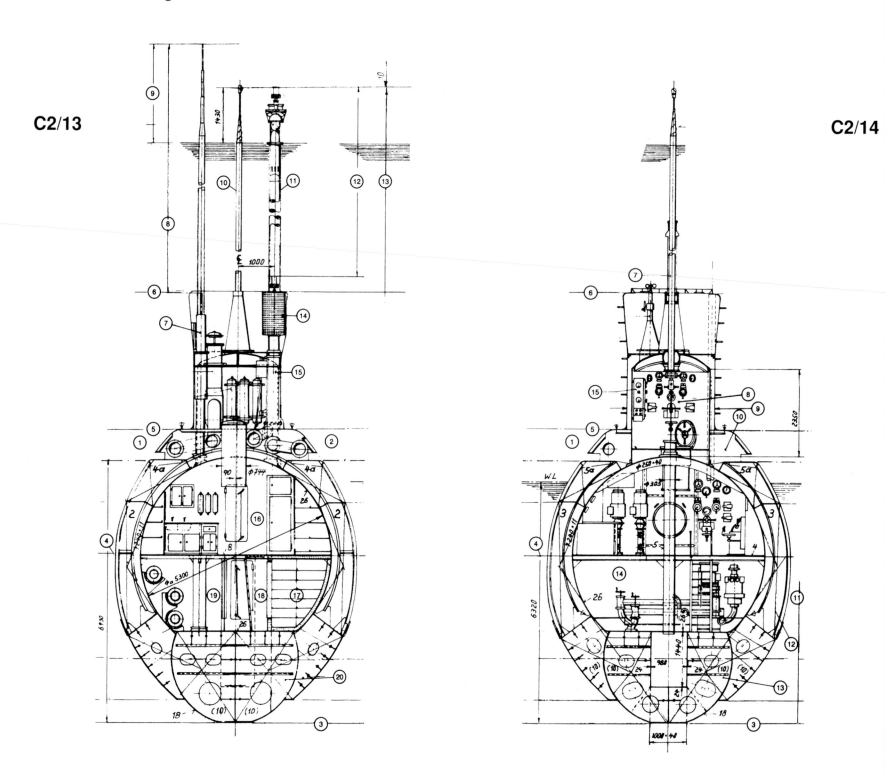

C2/13 Frame 34.4 looking forward

1 Port
2 Starboard
3 Base line (keel sole)
4 Datum line and pressure hull axis
5 Upper deck level
6 Roof of conning tower casing
7 Retractable rod aerial
8 Height above conning tower c6.200m
9 Height above waterline for radio reception c2.600m
10 Attack periscope
11 Schnorkel (raised)
12 Height (raised) 6.000m
13 Height above base line 17.686m

14 Schnorkel valve head (1943)
15 Schnorkel (lowered)
16 Galley
17 Freezer
18 Lobby
19 Magazine
20 Regulating tank 1 (port and starboard), frames 33.3 to 36.0 (13.08cu m each)

C2/14 Frame 37.6 looking forward

1 Port
2 Starboard
3 Base line (keel sole)
4 Datum line and pressure hull axis
5 Upper deck level
6 Roof of conning lower casing
7 Navigation periscope
8 Conning tower steering position
9 Width of conning tower 2.400m
10 Free-flooding space

11 Height 5.800m above base line
12 Diving tank 5 (port and starboard), frames 36.0 to 45.6 (21.63cu m each)
13 Regulating tank 2 (port and starboard), frames 36.0 to 38.4 (10.25cu m each)
14 Auxiliary machinery room
15 Torpedo calculator

C2/15 Frame 40.8 (auxiliary bulkhead) looking aft, looking on bulkhead 40.0

1 Starboard
2 Port
3 Base line (keel sole)
4 Datum line and pressure hull axis
5 Upper deck level
6 Bridge deck
7 Bridge deck height above pressure hull 2.669m
8 Conning tower roof height above base line 11.340m
9 Free-flooding space

10 Commander's quarters
11 Sickbay

C2/16 Frame 41.6 looking forward

1 Port
2 Starboard
3 Base line (keel sole)
4 Datum line and pressure hull axis
5 Upper deck level
6 Bridge deck, armoured against aircraft shells
7 Conning tower casing
8 Handrails
9 Forward container for inflatable liferaft
10 Radio room
11 Battery compartment 1.2
12 Battery compartment 2.2
13 Commander's quarters

C2/15

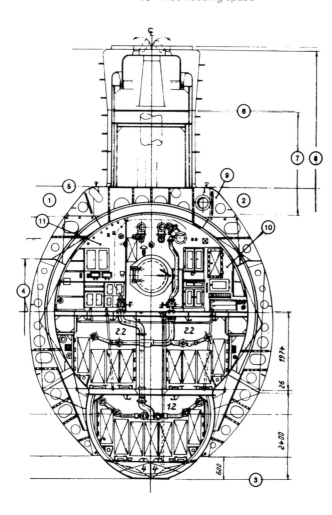

C2/16

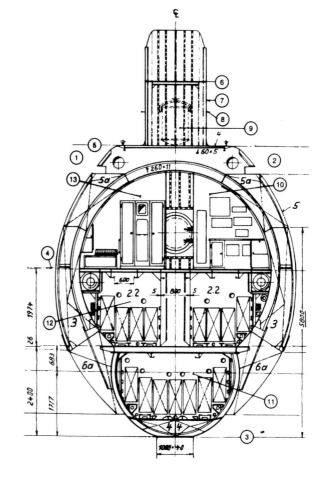

C Internal arrangement

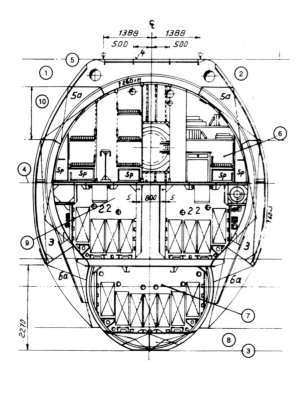

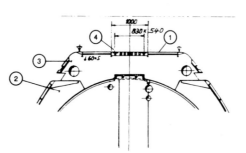

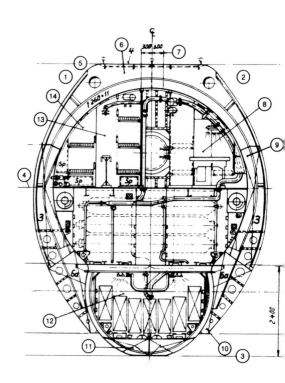

C2/17 Frame 44.0 looking forward

1 Port
2 Starboard
3 Base line (keel sole)
4 Datum line and pressure hull axis
5 Upper deck level
6 Chief engineer's quarters
7 Battery compartment 1.2
8 Ballast compartment 4
9 Battery compartment 2.2
10 Oil-tight bulkhead, frame 44.8

C2/18 Detail of frame 44.4, showing battery hatch

1 Upper deck
2 Fuel oil bunker 5a (port and starboard), frames 36.0 to 44.8 (8.15 cu m each)
3 Free-flooding space to frame 45.6

4 Battery hatch

C2/19 Frame 45.4 looking forward, looking on watertight bulkhead (above) and auxiliary bulkhead (below) at frame 45.6

1 Port
2 Starboard
3 Base line (keel sole)
4 Datum line and pressure hull axis
5 Upper deck level
6 Free-flooding space
7 Centre of diving tank 4 vent (at frame 46.0)
8 Officers' quarters
9 Diving tank 3 (port and starboard)
10 Fuel oil bunker 6a
11 Ballast compartment 4
12 Battery compartment 1.2

13 Senior ratings' quarters
14 Battery circuit breaker

100

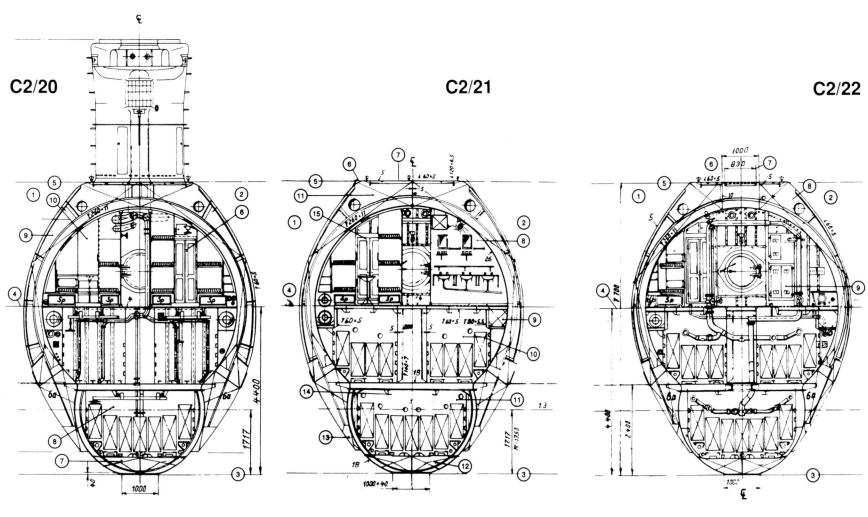

C2/20 **Frame 46.4 looking aft, looking on watertight bulkhead (above) and auxiliary bulkhead (below) at frame 45.6**

1 Starboard
2 Port
3 Base line (keel sole)
4 Datum line and pressure hull axis
5 Upper deck level
6 Petty officers' quarters
7 Ballast compartment 4 (sealed)
8 Battery compartment 1.3
9 Diving tank 4 (port and starboard)
10 Officers' quarters

C2/21 **Frame 49.6 looking forward**

1 Port
2 Starboard

3 Base line (keel sole)
4 Datum line and pressure hull axis
5 Upper deck level
6 Designed break of hull plating
7 Support bulkhead at frame 48.8
8 Wash room
9 Dirty water tank
10 Battery compartment 2.3
11 Battery compartment 1.3
12 Ballast compartment 4
13 Fuel oil bunker 6a (port and starboard)
14 Rails for battery inspection trolley
15 Petty officers' quarters
16 Diving tank 4

C2/22 **Frame 51.2 looking forward, looking on bulkhead 52.1**

1 Port
2 Starboard

3 Base line (keel sole)
4 Datum line and pressure hull axis
5 Upper deck level
6 Oil-tight longitudinal bulkhead
7 Torpedo hatch
8 Diving tank 4 (port and starboard)
9 Battery circuit breaker

C2/23

C2/24

C2/26

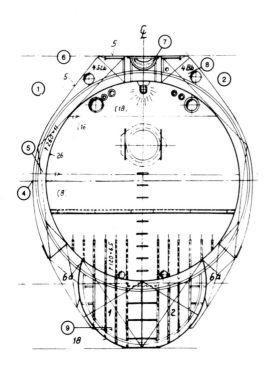

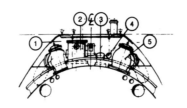

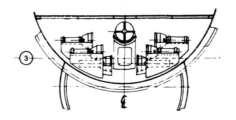

C2/25

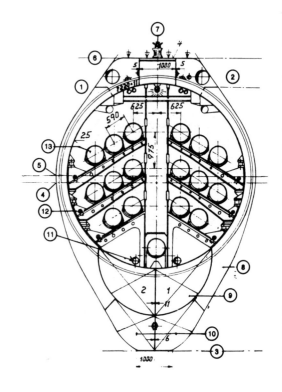

C2/23 Frame 52.4 looking aft, looking on auxiliary bulkhead 52.0 and pressure bulkhead 52.1

1 Starboard
2 Port
3 Base line (keel sole)
4 Datum line
5 Pressure hull axis
6 Upper deck level
7 Torpedo loading channel
8 Diving tank 4 (port and starboard)
9 Torpedo compensating tanks (port and starboard

C2/24 Detail of frame 57.2 looking forward

1 Free-flooding space
2 Forward hydroplane drive motor

3 Bevel gears for hydroplane
4 Vent for diving tank 5
5 Exhaust valve for diving tank 5

C2/25 Detail of frame 52.4 looking forward, showing one reload torpedo and eighteen torpedo warhead pistols

C2/26 Frame 56.8 looking forward, looking on oil-tight bulkhead (above)

1 Port
2 Starboard
3 Base line (keel sole)
4 Datum line
5 Pressure hull axis
6 Upper deck level

7 Capstan (removeable)
8 Fuel oil bunker 7a (port and starboard), frames 52.8 to 58.6 (18.95cu m each)
9 Torpedo compensating tanks (port and starboard), frames 52.0 to 58.8 (13.65cu m each)
10 Ballast compartment 5 (sealed) frames 53.6 to 58.4 (8.43cu m)
11 Piping to trimming tanks 3 (starboard) and 4 (port)
12 Worm-drive for torpedo reload mechanism
13 Reload torpedo magazine

C2/27

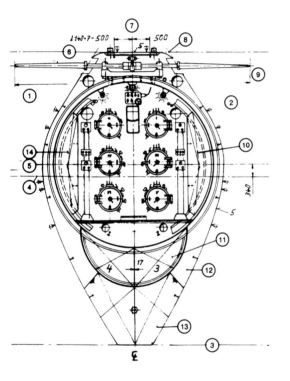

C2/28

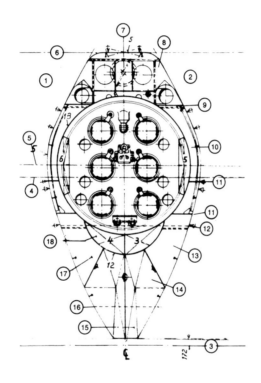

C2/29

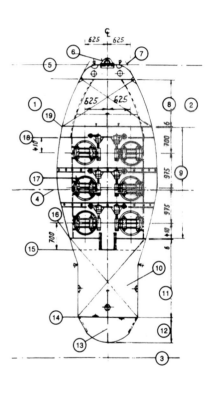

C2/27 Frame 59.6 (auxiliary bulkhead) looking forward

1 Port
2 Starboard
3 Base line (keel sole)
4 Datum line
5 Pressure hull axis
6 Upper deck level
7 Centre of deck cleats, frame 59.8
8 Projected break of hull plating
9 Forward hydroplane fully extended (3.205m to centreline)
10 Torpedo compensating tanks for tubes, 1, 3 and 5, frames 60.2 to 62.4
11 Trimming tanks 3 and 4 (pressure-tight), frames 58.8 to 62.4 (3.60cu m each)
12 Free-flooding space
13 Ballast compartment 6 (sealed),

frames 58.8 to 62.4 (14.00cu m)
14 Torpedo compensating tanks for tubes 2, 4 and 6, frames 60.2 to 62.4

C2/28 Frame 62.4 looking forward, showing support bulkhead (above) and watertight bulkhead (below)

1 Port
2 Starboard
3 Base line (keel sole)
4 Datum line
5 Pressure hull axis
6 Upper deck level
7 Deck gratings, frames 62.4 to 63.84
8 Supporting bulkhead
9 Upper deck (inside casing)
10 End wall of diving tank 5
11 Edge of plating

12 Lower deck
13 Watertight bulkhead
14 Diving tank 5
15 Ballast compartments 6 (starboard) and 7 (port) (sealed)
16 Watertight ballast compartment deck
17 Free-flooding space
18 Trimming tanks 3 and 4 (pressure tight), frames 58.8 to 62.4 (3.60cu m each)

C2/29 Torpedo tube support bulkhead 67.415 and 67.631 looking aft

1 Starboard
2 Port
3 Base line (keel sole)
4 Datum line
5 Upper deck level
6 Towing eye

7 Projected break of hull plating
8 Watertight forecastle
9 Free-flooding space
10 Watertight bulkhead
11 Ballast compartment
12 GHG sound detection apparatus
13 GHG balcony
14 Watertight GHG balcony deck
15 Lower deck level
16 A deck
17 Torpedo tube outer doors
18 F deck
19 Upper deck (inside casing)

C Internal arrangement

C3   **TYPE XXI (1944) REVISED LAYOUT OF RADIO ROOM (no scale)**

C3/1   **Gatefold elevation looking on inboard bulkhead**

C3/2   **Elevation of outboard side**

C3/3   **Plan**

1   Radio direction finder repeater
2   Junction box for RDF repeater
3   RDF superheterodyne receiver
4   RDF aerial socket
5   Mains equipment
6   Switch box (2)
7   Wall socket (5)
8   Pin sockets
9   Short wave receiver (2)
10   All-waveband receiver
11   10W ultra-short wave receiver
12   10W ultra-short wave mains equipment
13   Controls for short wave transmitter
14   Unidentified controls
15   200W short wave transmitter
16   40W short wave transmitter
17   Transmitter aerial selector
18   Receiver aerial selector
19   Mains switchboard
20   Coding/decoding equipment
21   Auxiliary apparatus for coding/decoding equipment
22   Mains apparatus for coding/decoding equipment
23   Lower deck loudspeaker
24   Branch circuit socket
25   Interchangeable cabin lamp
26   Radio telephone switchbox
27   RT volume control
28   Radio telephone
29   Co-listening socket
30   Additional pin socket
31   Security locker
32   Ceiling lamp with switch
33   Socket with switch
34   Branch circuit socket (coding/decoding equipment)
35   Ultra-short wave receiver loudspeaker volume control

C3/1

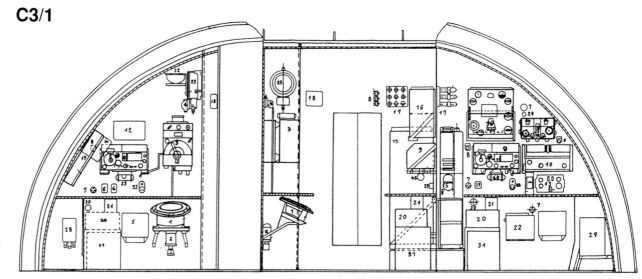

C3/2

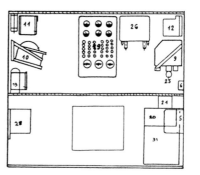

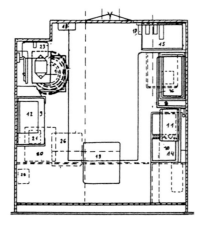

C3/3

D1/1

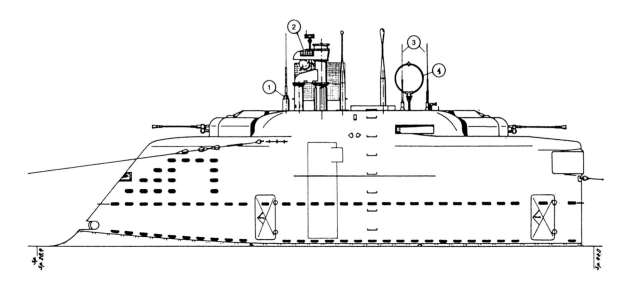

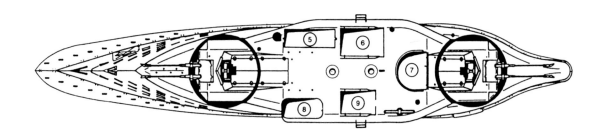

D1/2

D1 **TYPE XXI (1944) TYPICAL EXTERNAL APPEARANCE OF CONNING TOWER (1/100 scale)**

D1/1 Starboard elevation, showing schnorkel and retractable aerials

D1/2 Plan showing schnorkel, retractable aerials and bridge watch positions

1 Retractable rod aerial
2 Schnorkel with 'Bali I' radar detector aerial
3 VHF dipoles
4 Radio direction finder
5 'Hohentwiel U' radar transmitter/receiver aerial
6 Port bridge watch station
7 Surface steering position
8 Schnorkel
9 Starboard bridge watch position

D Conning tower

D1/3 Starboard elevation, showing schnorkel extended

1 After jumping wire (port and starboard)
2 Detachable guardrail
3 Sliphook
4 Stern light
5 Anti-aircraft turret with twin 2cm Flak C38 (3cm Flak M44 in double CM44 mounting as designed)
6 Door to galley hatch
7 Schnorkel head valve with radar-absorbent cladding (various types)
8 FuMB Ant 3 'Bali I' radar detection aerial
9 Schnorkel diesel exhaust
10 Schnorkel diesel air intake
11 Attack periscope
12 Navigation periscope
13 Masthead light (detachable)
14 Lifebelt
15 Searchlight (port)
16 Bridge access ladder to deck
17 Radio direction finder aerial
18 VHF dipole (starboard)
19 SU sonar equipment
20 Forward casing door
21 Starboard navigation light

D1/3

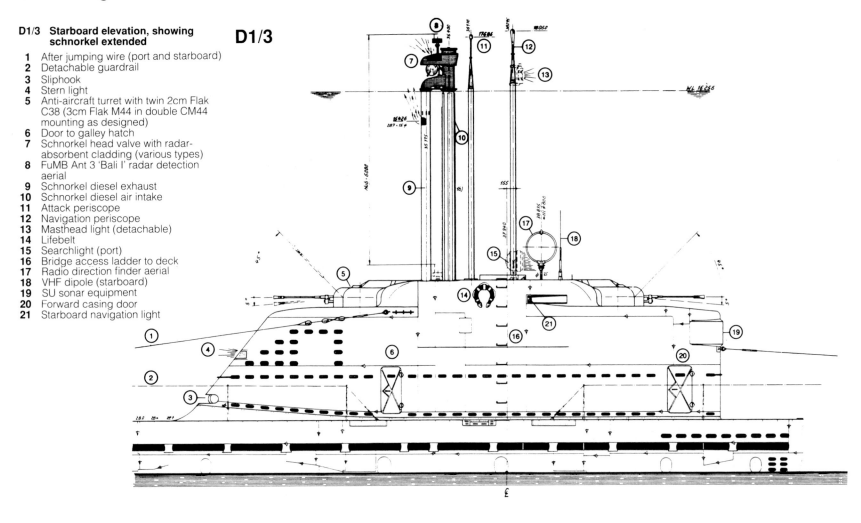

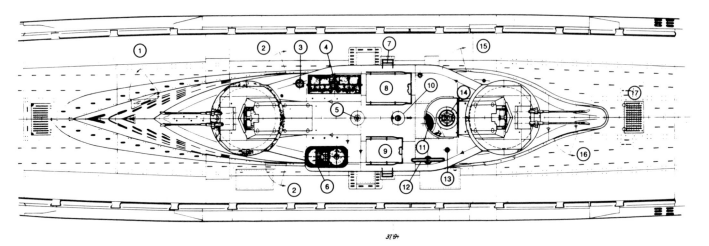

D1/4

D1/5

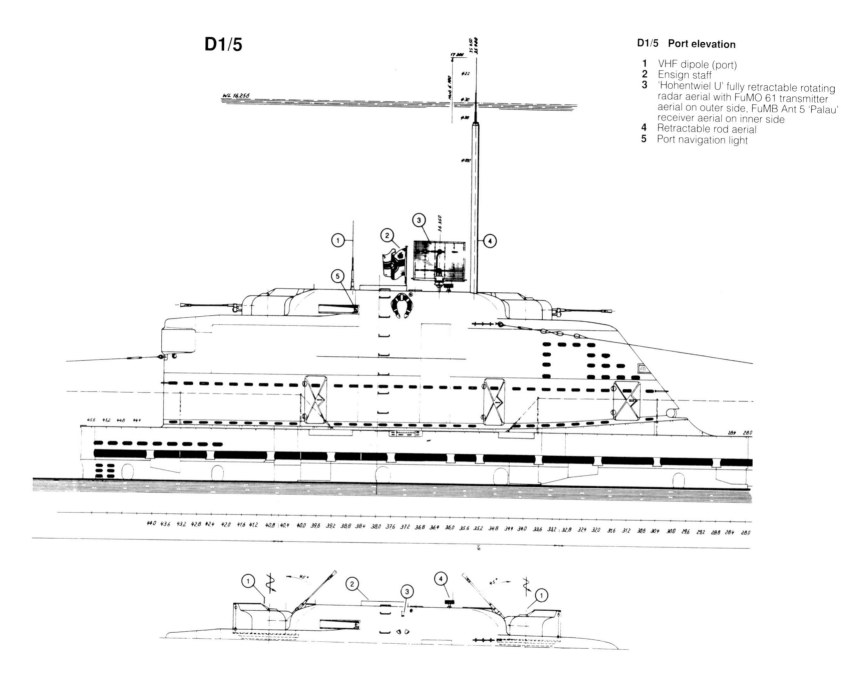

D1/5 Port elevation

1 VHF dipole (port)
2 Ensign staff
3 'Hohentwiel U' fully retractable rotating radar aerial with FuMO 61 transmitter aerial on outer side, FuMB Ant 5 'Palau' receiver aerial on inner side
4 Retractable rod aerial
5 Port navigation light

D1/4 Plan

1 After casing door (access to inflatable liferaft)
2 Doors to galley hatch
3 Retractable rod aerial
4 'Hohentwiel U' fully retractable rotating radar aerial
5 Attack periscope
6 Schnorkel with 'Bali I' radar detection aerial
7 Bridge access ladder to deck
8 Port bridge watch station
9 Starboard bridge watch station
10 Navigation periscope
11 Surface steering position
12 Radio direction finder aerial (retractable)
13 VHF dipoles
14 UZO surface torpedo-aiming equipment
15 Casing door
16 Forward casing door
17 Battery hatch

D1/6

D1/6 Port elevation detail, showing 2cm flak turrets at 180° traverse

1 Turret axis of rotation
2 Spray protector for bridge watch position
3 Mounting points for lifebelt
4 'Bali I' radar detection aerial on schnorkel in fully retracted position

D Conning tower

D1/7 Forward elevation

1 Lifebelt
2 Radio direction finder aerial (retractable)
3 VHF dipoles (rubberized)
4 UZO surface torpedo-aiming equipment
5 Navigation lights (port and starboard)
6 Free-flooding space
7 Conning tower
8 Pressure hull

D1/8 Forward elevation of conning tower top, showing navigation periscope raised

1 Navigation lights (port and starboard)
2 Navigation periscope

D1/9 Aft elevation

1 'Hohentwiel U' radar aerial
2 FuMB Ant 5 'Palau' receiver aerial
3 FuMO 61 radar transmitter aerial
4 Schnorkel with radar-absorbent cladding on head
5 Access hatch to anti-aircraft turret

6 Lifebelt
7 Stern light
8 Sliphook
9 Free-flooding space
10 Pressure hull
11 Conning tower
12 After casing door (access to inflatable liferaft)
13 Section of schnorkel at I–I
14 Toothed rack
15 Intake pipe 319mm in diameter
16 Exhaust pipe 267mm in diameter

D1/10 Aft elevation of conning tower top, showing attack periscope support raised

1 Ensign standard
2 Attack periscope, partially fitted with radar-absorbent cladding
3 Commander's pennant

D1/11 Detail of 'Hohentwiel U' aerial

1 FuMO 61 radar transmitter aerial
2 FuMB Ant 5 'Palau' receiver aerial

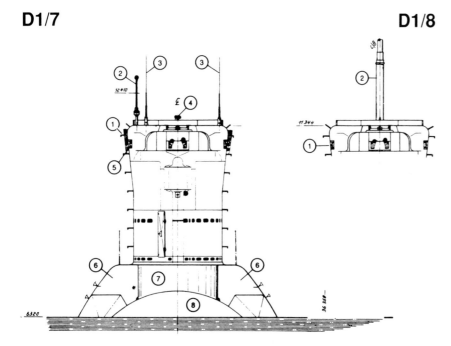

D1/7   **D1/8**   **D1/9**   **D1/10**

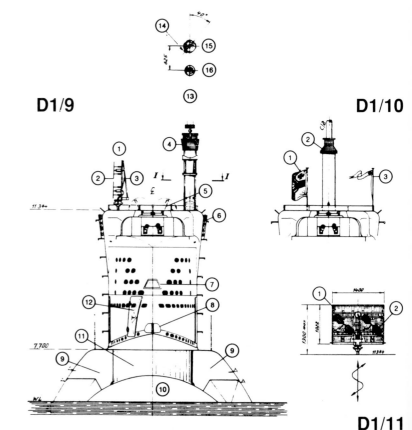

D1/11

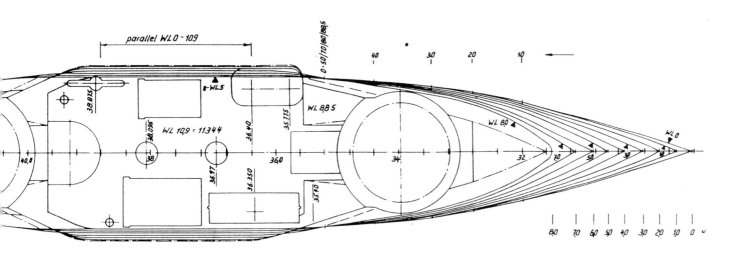

D2/2 Lines from aft

D2/3 Lines from forward

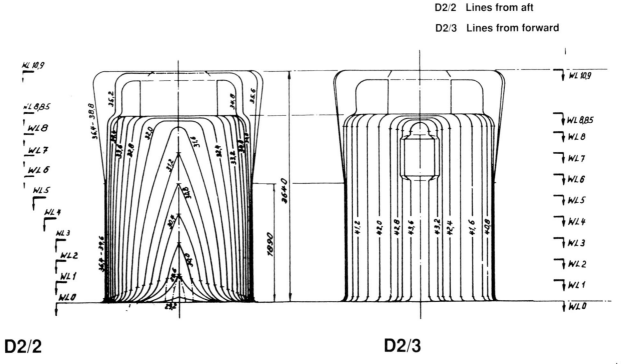

D2/2   **D2/3**

D Conning tower

D3/1

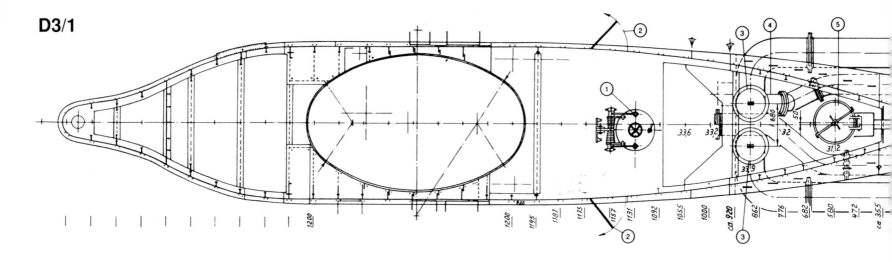

D3/2

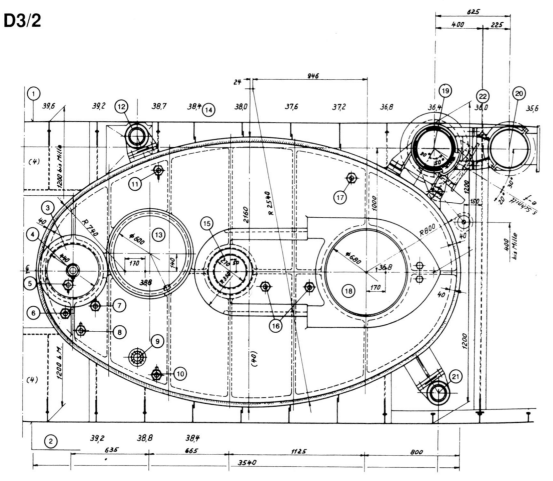

**D3/2 Plan of section 5 inside casing
(1/30 scale)**

1 Conning tower casing (starboard side)
2 Conning tower casing (port side)
3 UZO surface torpedo-aiming
   equipment
4 Aperture for UZO transmission shaft
5 Aperture for UZO torpedo-firing cable
6 Aperture for heater for UZO optical
   equipment
7 Aperture for heater for UZO
   transmission
8 Aperture for bearing compass
   repeater
9 Aperture for speaking tube
10 Aperture for port navigation light
11 Aperture for starboard navigation light
12 Radio direction finder mounting
13 Conning tower hatch
14 Support bulkhead
15 Navigation periscope mounting
16 Aperture for periscope greasing points
17 Aperture for welding equipment
    connection
18 Attack periscope
19 Schnorkel air intake pipe
20 Schnorkel exhaust pipe
21 Retractable radar aerial mounting
22 Support bulkhead

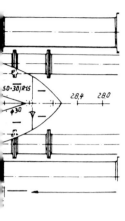

D3 TYPE XXI (1943) CONNING TOWER AND SCHNORKEL DETAILS

D3/1 Plan of casing, showing air intake and ventilator trunking for surface running (1/60 scale)

1 Galley hatch (fitted with easing spring)
2 Door in casing (access to galley hatch)
3 Diesel air intake heads for surface running
4 Air intake connection and trunking for room ventilators
5 Pressure-resistant container for 5-man inflatable liferaft

D3/4 Section of hull from aft, showing schnorkel and periscope wells (1/60 scale)

1 Keel sole
2 Base line
3 Lower axis
4 Lower deck
5 Datum line (main deck level)
6 Height 2.270m above base line
7 Height 2.400m above base line
8 Height 5.800m above base line
9 Height 6.900m above base line
10 Centreline of attack periscope well
11 Provision store
12 Pressure-tight downtake from air intake
13 Central control room (upper level)
14 Fuel oil bunker 5 (starboard)
15 Diving tank 3 (starboard)
16 Potato locker (central control room lower level aft)
17 Regulating tank 2 (starboard)
18 Regulating bunker 1 (starboard)

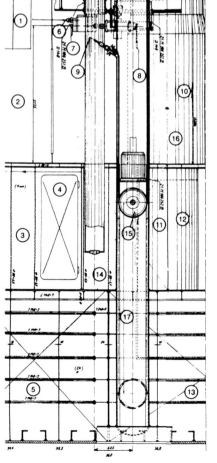

D3/3

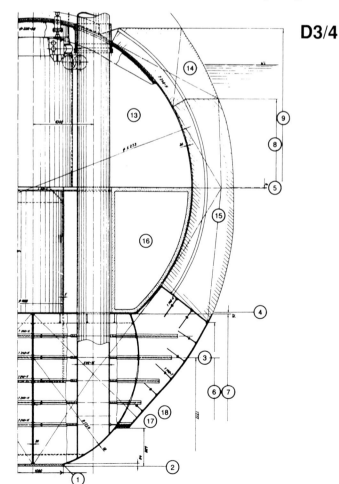

D3/4

D3/3 Section of hull from starboard, showing schnorkel and periscope wells (1/60 scale)

1 Galley hatch (frame 34.39)
2 Galley
3 Lobby
4 Door to magazine
5 Regulating bunker 1 (starboard)
6 Compressed air connection
7 Compressed air inlet control lever (to raise schnorkel)
8 Brake lever for schnorkel raising mechanism
9 'Bali I' radar detector aerial connection
10 Central control room (upper level)
11 Provision store
12 Central control room (lower level)
13 Regulating tank 2 (starboard)
14 Water outlet to bilges
15 Counterweight for radar detector aerial cable
16 Centreline of attack periscope well
17 Half-height

D Conning tower

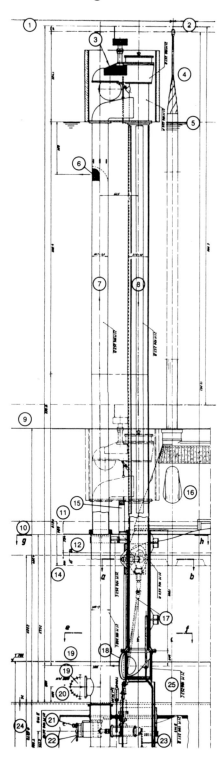

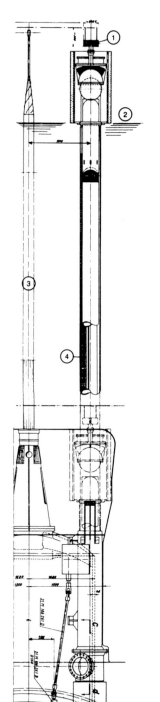

D3/5 Section of conning tower from starboard, showing details of schnorkel and periscope (1/60 scale)

1 Distance from frame station 1, 36.907m
2 Distance to centreline of navigation periscope, 1.125m
3 Air intake head
4 Schnorkelling only with raised attack periscope
5 Waterline when schnorkelling
6 Exhaust gas outlet
7 Diesel exhaust tube
8 Diesel air intake tube
9 Upper edge of casing 11.340m above base line
10 Bridge deck
11 Upper limit of conning tower ceiling (domed)
12 Datum line
13 Upper edge of conning tower
14 Lower limit of conning tower ceiling
15 Buffer for retracted schnorkel
16 Periscope shelter
17 Schnorkel raising mechanism (compressed air driven, with bevel gear transmission)
18 Air intake flange
19 Intake flange from diesel exhaust gas trunking
20 Pressure hull
21 Compressed air connection
22 Compressed air inlet control lever
23 Brake lever for schnorkel raising mechanism
24 All measurements to base line
25 Centreline of attack periscope

D3/6 Section of conning tower from aft, showing details of schnorkel and periscope (1/60 scale)

1 FuMO 'Bali I' radar detector aerial
2 Waterline when schnorkelling
3 Centreline of attack periscope, conning tower and U-boat
4 Gear rack for schnorkel raising mechanism

D3/5   **D3/6**

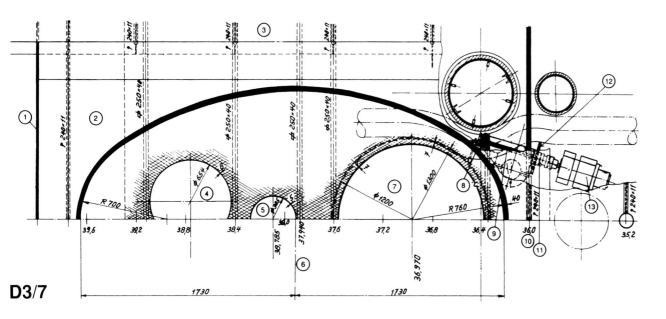

D3/7

D3/7 Part plan of conning tower ceiling
at g–h in drawing D3/5 (1/30 scale)

1 Auxiliary bulkhead 40.0
2 Pressure hull
3 Fuel oil bunker 5a
4 Conning tower hatch
5 Navigation periscope
6 Athwartship centreline of conning
tower
7 Attack periscope
8 Brake for schnorkel raising mechanism
9 Worm drive
10 Support bulkhead
11 Clutch
12 Chain wheel for manual raising of
schnorkel
13 Compressed air drive motor

D3/8 Sectional plan e–f inside conning
tower casing, showing schnorkel
trunking connections (see
drawing D3/5) (1/30 scale)

1 Galley hatch
2 Conning tower casing – interior
3 Schnorkel air intake valve
4 Conning tower casing
5 Support bulkhead
6 Centreline of U-boat
7 Conning tower

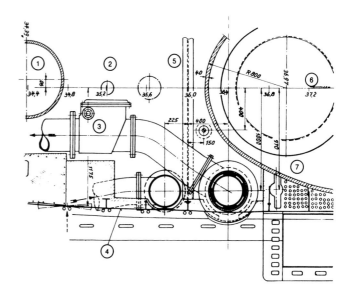

D3/8

D Conning tower

D3/9

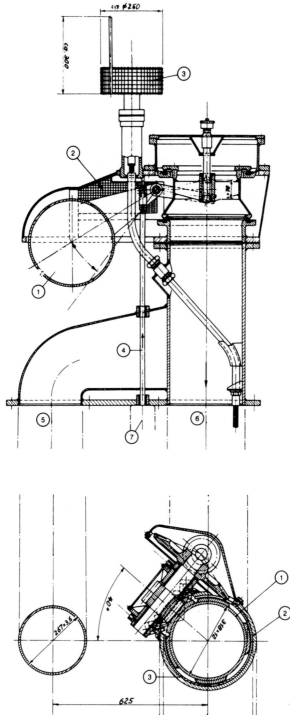

D3/9 Detail of schnorkel ball float and head valve (1/15 scale)

1 Ball float (shown in closed position)
2 Air intake
3 FuMB Ant 3 'Bali I' radar detector aerial (broad-band circular horizontal/vertical aerial, 100–400 MHz)
4 Remote control rod for intake/exhaust head valves
5 Exhaust tube
6 Air intake tube
7 Buffer

D3/10 Section a–b, detail of schnorkel air intake tube and bevel gear drive (see drawing D3/5) (1/15 scale)

1 Air intake tube
2 Housing for intake tube
3 Guide bushes at top and bottom only

D3/11 Sectional profile c–d of schnorkel base air inlet (see drawing D3/6) (1/15 scale)

1 Air intake connection from schnorkel
2 Pressure-tight housing

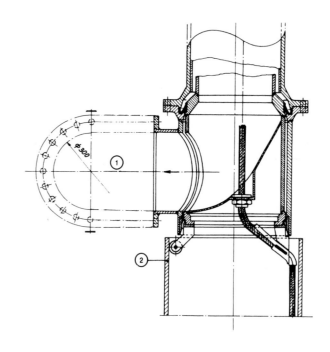

D3/10

D3/11

114

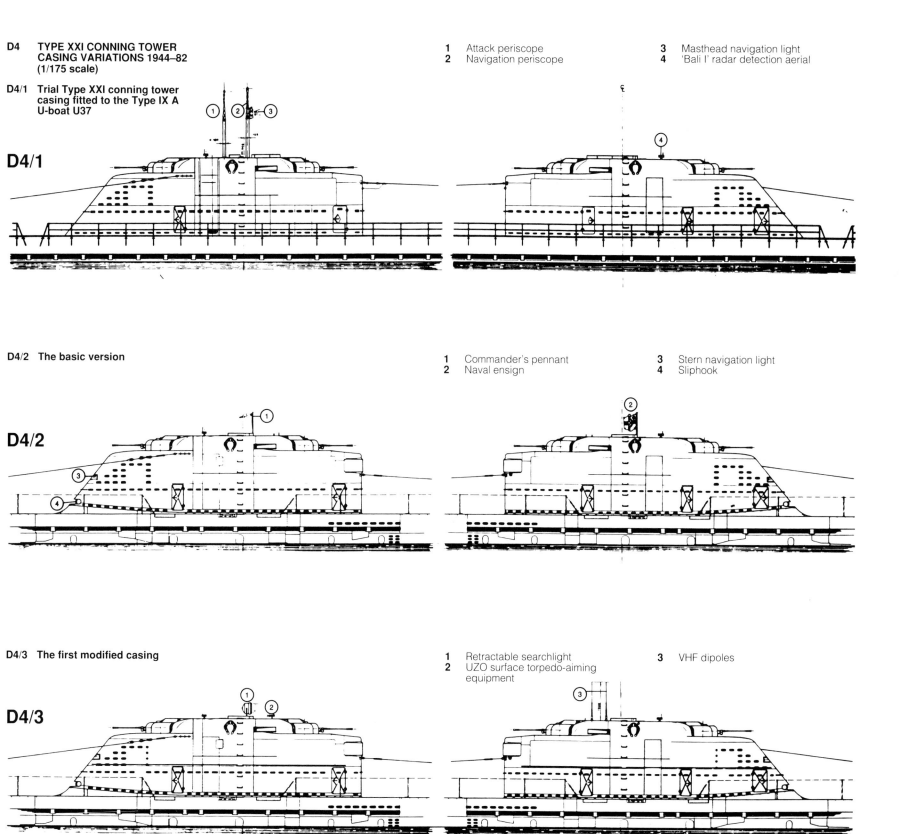

D4 **TYPE XXI CONNING TOWER CASING VARIATIONS 1944–82** (1/175 scale)

D4/1 **Trial Type XXI conning tower casing fitted to the Type IX A U-boat U37**

1 Attack periscope
2 Navigation periscope
3 Masthead navigation light
4 'Bali I' radar detection aerial

D4/1

D4/2 **The basic version**

1 Commander's pennant
2 Naval ensign
3 Stern navigation light
4 Sliphook

D4/2

D4/3 **The first modified casing**

1 Retractable searchlight
2 UZO surface torpedo-aiming equipment
3 VHF dipoles

D4/3

115

D Conning tower

D4/4   The first casing as built on U2501

1   Radio direction finder aerial
2   'Hohentwiel U' radar transmitter/
    receiver aerial

D4/4

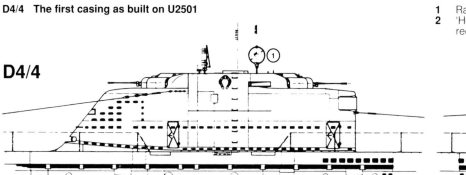
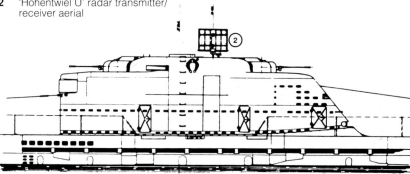

D4/5   The second version

1   'Hohentwiel U' aerial inner side
2   Height of 'Hohentwiel U' aerial 1.305m
    max
3   Flak turret with twin 30mm M44–U anti-
    aircraft guns (as designed)
4   Flak turret with twin 20mm Flak 38 M II
    anti-aircraft guns (as built)
5   Schnorkel support, shown in raised
    (schnorkelling) position

D4/5

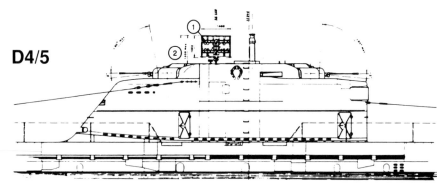
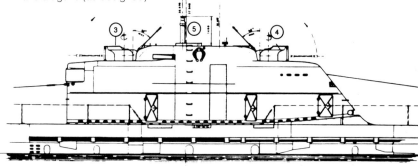

**D4/6   The Type XXI casing shown at
schnorkel depth, also showing the
periscope field of vision**

1   Schnorkel with 'Bali I' radar detector
    aerial
2   Navigation periscope angle of vision
3   Schnorkel air intake head
4   Exhaust tube
5   Air intake tube
6   Navigation periscope (raised)
7   Attack periscope angle of vision
8   Attack periscope (raised)
9   'Bali I' radar detector aerial
10 Retractable rod aerial

D4/6

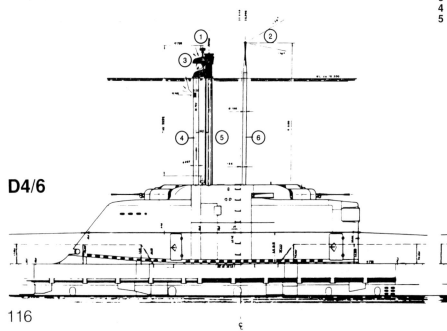
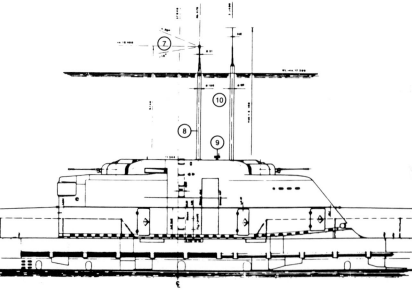

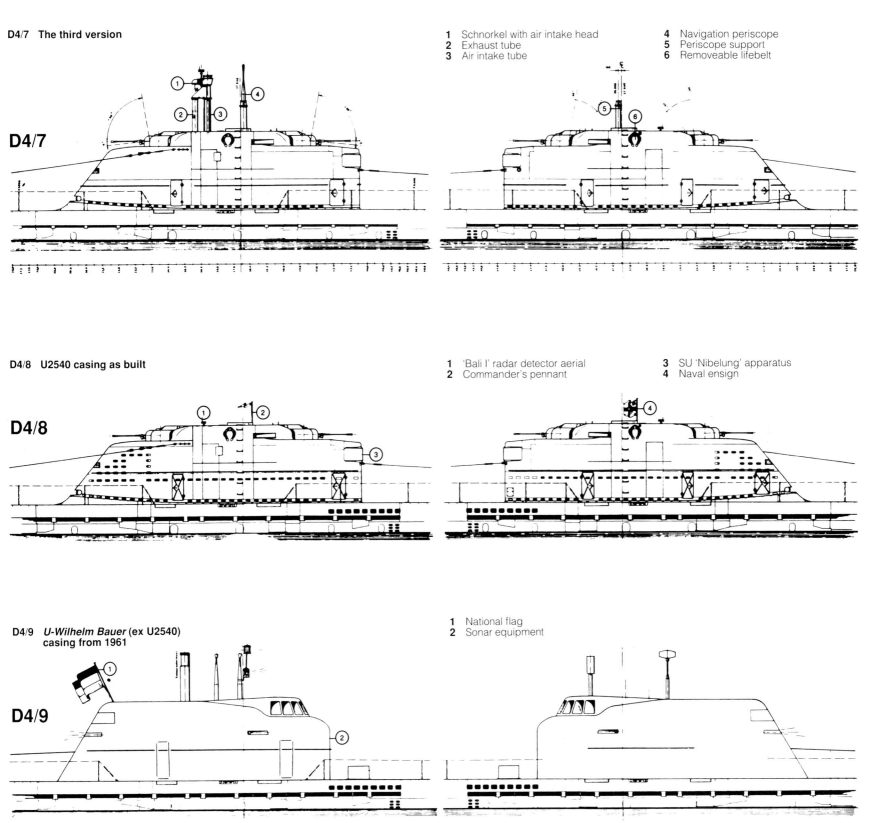

D4/7 The third version

1 Schnorkel with air intake head
2 Exhaust tube
3 Air intake tube
4 Navigation periscope
5 Periscope support
6 Removeable lifebelt

D4/7

D4/8 U2540 casing as built

1 'Bali I' radar detector aerial
2 Commander's pennant
3 SU 'Nibelung' apparatus
4 Naval ensign

D4/8

D4/9 *U-Wilhelm Bauer* (ex U2540) casing from 1961

1 National flag
2 Sonar equipment

D4/9

D Conning tower

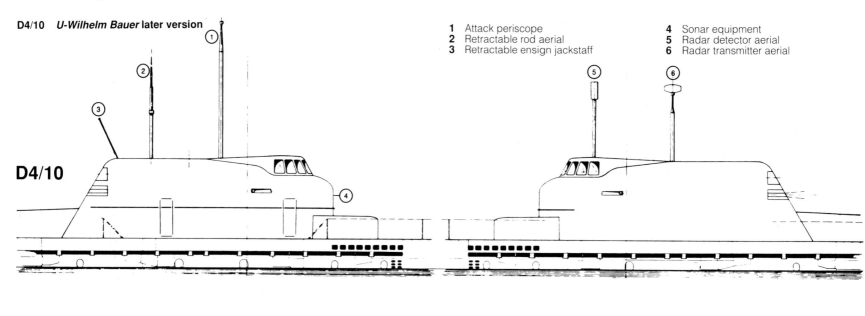

D4/10 *U-Wilhelm Bauer* later version

1 Attack periscope
2 Retractable rod aerial
3 Retractable ensign jackstaff
4 Sonar equipment
5 Radar detector aerial
6 Radar transmitter aerial

D4/10

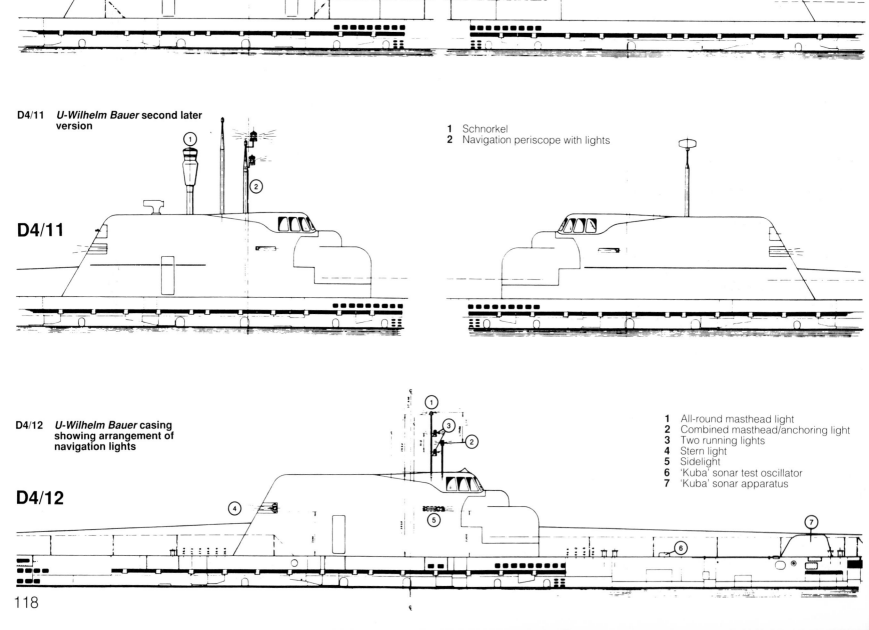

D4/11 *U-Wilhelm Bauer* second later version

1 Schnorkel
2 Navigation periscope with lights

D4/11

D4/12 *U-Wilhelm Bauer* casing showing arrangement of navigation lights

1 All-round masthead light
2 Combined masthead/anchoring light
3 Two running lights
4 Stern light
5 Sidelight
6 'Kuba' sonar test oscillator
7 'Kuba' sonar apparatus

D4/12

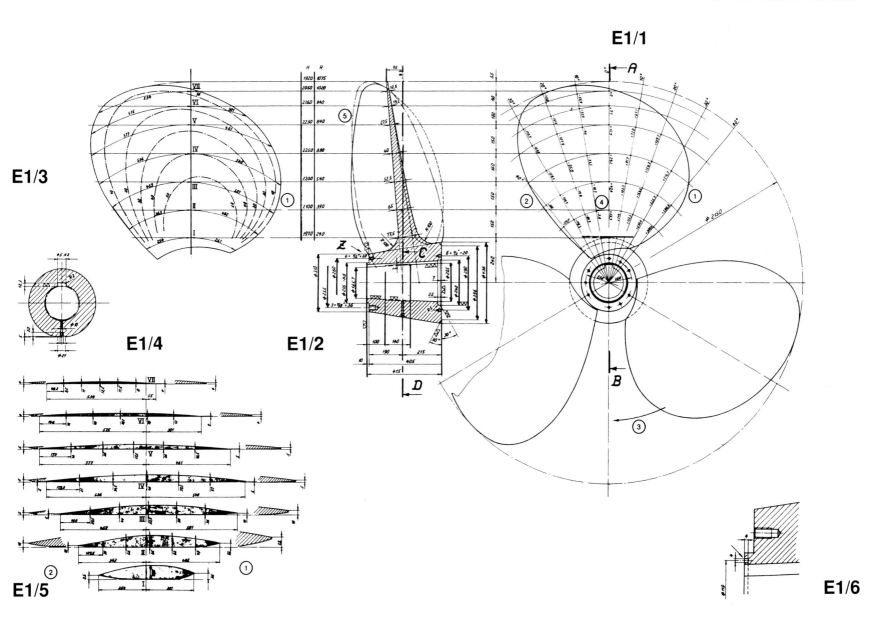

E1/1

E1/3

E1/4   E1/2

E1/5

E1/6

E1	**PROPELLER** **(1/20 scale except as marked)**
E1/1	**Profile**
E1/2	**Section A–B**
E1/3	**Profile of blade**
E1/4	**Section C–D (propeller hub)**
E1/5	**Sections of typical blade**
E1/6	**Detail section of point Z (junction** **of blade and hub flange)** **(1/5 scale)**

1 Leading edge of blade
2 Trailing edge of blade
3 Direction of rotation (ahead)
4 Pitch variations
5 Curve of penetration

Details of propeller:

Diameter	2.150m
Pitch at centre	2.110m
Developed blade area	2.220sq m
Number of blades	3
Direction of rotation	port – anti-clockwise; starboard – clockwise
Material	Steel 45.81 8K
Weight	850Kg ± 5%
Design	OKM – Berlin, Department KIIE d 3

E Selected details

E2 JUNKERS 4 FK 115 AIR COMPRESSOR, RATED AT 101/min AT 200atm (1/20 scale)

1 Exhaust pipe (90mm steel pipe)
2 Cooling water outlet pipe (22mm)
3 Cooling water inlet pipe (22mm)
4 High pressure air output pipe (16mm)

E3/1

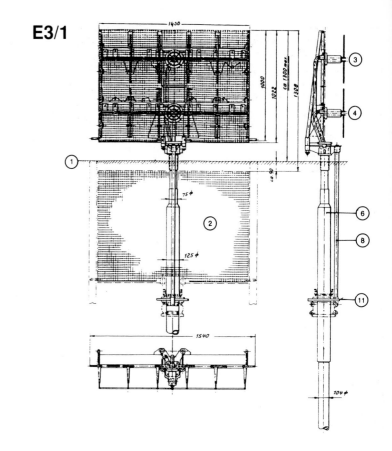

E2

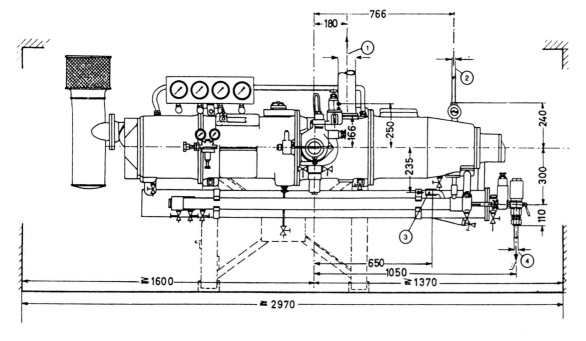

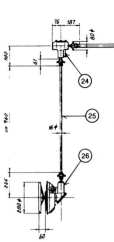

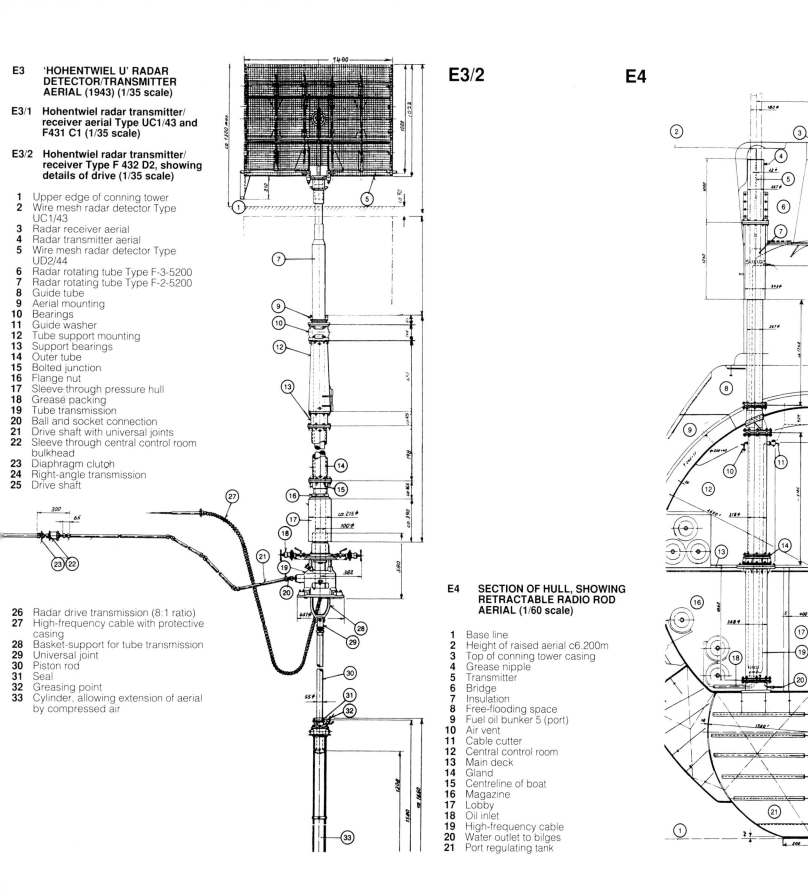

E3 'HOHENTWIEL U' RADAR DETECTOR/TRANSMITTER AERIAL (1943) (1/35 scale)

E3/1 Hohentwiel radar transmitter/receiver aerial Type UC1/43 and F431 C1 (1/35 scale)

E3/2 Hohentwiel radar transmitter/receiver Type F 432 D2, showing details of drive (1/35 scale)

1   Upper edge of conning tower
2   Wire mesh radar detector Type UC1/43
3   Radar receiver aerial
4   Radar transmitter aerial
5   Wire mesh radar detector Type UD2/44
6   Radar rotating tube Type F-3-5200
7   Radar rotating tube Type F-2-5200
8   Guide tube
9   Aerial mounting
10 Bearings
11 Guide washer
12 Tube support mounting
13 Support bearings
14 Outer tube
15 Bolted junction
16 Flange nut
17 Sleeve through pressure hull
18 Grease packing
19 Tube transmission
20 Ball and socket connection
21 Drive shaft with universal joints
22 Sleeve through central control room bulkhead
23 Diaphragm clutch
24 Right-angle transmission
25 Drive shaft

26 Radar drive transmission (8:1 ratio)
27 High-frequency cable with protective casing
28 Basket-support for tube transmission
29 Universal joint
30 Piston rod
31 Seal
32 Greasing point
33 Cylinder, allowing extension of aerial by compressed air

E3/2

E4

E4   SECTION OF HULL, SHOWING RETRACTABLE RADIO ROD AERIAL (1/60 scale)

1   Base line
2   Height of raised aerial c6.200m
3   Top of conning tower casing
4   Grease nipple
5   Transmitter
6   Bridge
7   Insulation
8   Free-flooding space
9   Fuel oil bunker 5 (port)
10 Air vent
11 Cable cutter
12 Central control room
13 Main deck
14 Gland
15 Centreline of boat
16 Magazine
17 Lobby
18 Oil inlet
19 High-frequency cable
20 Water outlet to bilges
21 Port regulating tank

F U-Wilhelm Bauer

F1

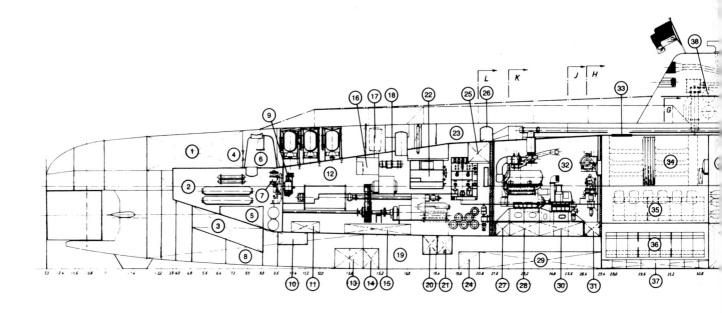

F2

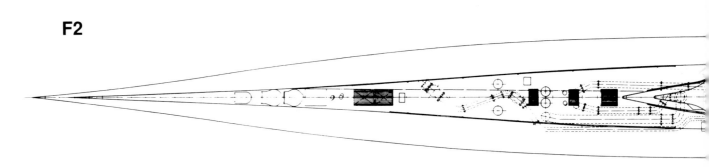

122

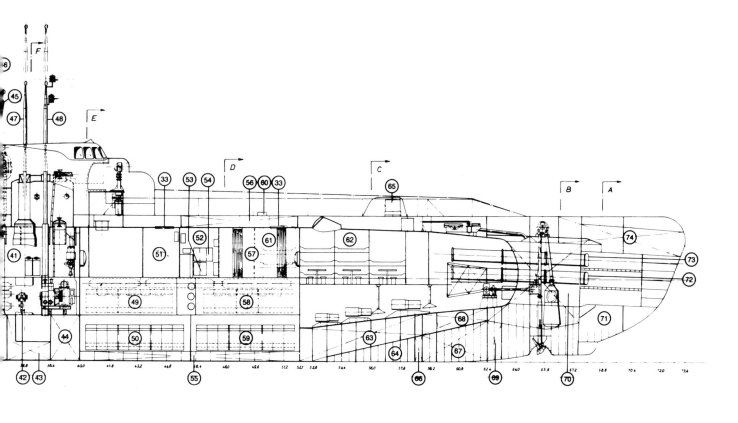

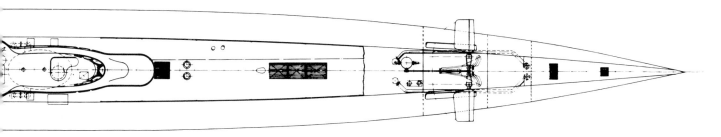

57	Officers' mess and accommodation for research personnel	
58	Battery compartment VI 4	
59	Battery compartment VI 3	
60	'Kuba' sonar test oscillator	
61	STO room	
62	Bow room (forward accommodation)	
63	Torpedo compensating tanks (port and starboard)	
64	Ballast compartment 5 (sealed)	
65	'Kuba' sonar equipment	
66	High-pressure water tank	
67	Ballast compartment 6 (sealed)	
68	Trimming tanks (port and starboard)	
69	Ballast compartment 7 (adjustable)	
70	Diving tank 5	

71 Ballast compartment
72 'Ablauf' torpedo tubes
73 Torpedo tubes
74 Watertight forecastle

F2   **PLAN (1/200 scale)**

F3

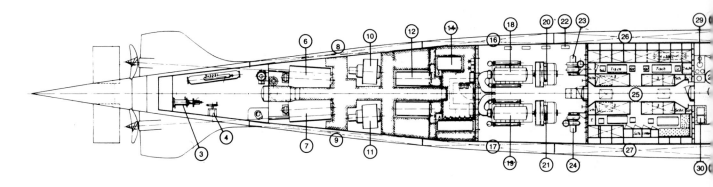

F4

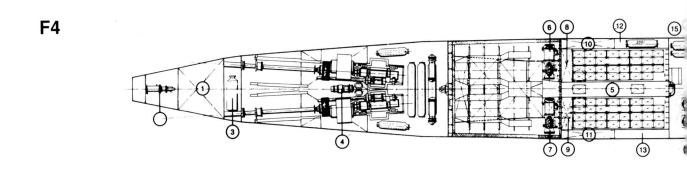

F3	**PLAN AT MAIN DECK**
	(1/200 scale)

1 Stern compartment
2 Two oxygen cylinders
3 Rudder drive
4 'Bold' asdic decoy ejector
5 Electric motor room
6 Port electric motor
7 Starboard electric motor
8 Fuel bunker 2 (port)
9 Fuel bunker 2 (starboard)
10 Port silent-running motor
11 Starboard silent-running motor
12 Port main switchboard
13 Starboard main switchboard
14 Generator switchboard
15 Auxiliary switchboard for main motors
16 Diving tank 1 (port)
17 Diving tank 1 (starboard)
18 Port main diesel engine
19 Starboard main diesel engine
20 Port generator
21 Starboard generator
22 Four air purifiers (Co2-absorbing)
23 Engineroom exhaust fan
24 Engineroom ventilating fan
25 Crew accommodation (*schr* (*Schranke*) = locker; *Tisch* = table; *Kst* (*Kasten*) = box locker)

26 Diving tank 2 (port)
27 Diving tank 2 (starboard)
28 Galley
29 Hot plates
30 Refrigerator
31 Locker
32 Provision store
33 Central control room
34 Radar mast
35 Schnorkel and periscope
36 Radar screen
37 Steering control for silent-running motors
38 Hydroplane controls
39 High-pressure oil pumps
40 Diving tank 3 (port)
41 Diving tank 3 (starboard)
42 Commander's quarters
43 Radio room
44 Location and sensing research room
45 GHG apparatus
46 'Kuba' sonar operating equipment
47 Panorama scanning equipment
48 M1H sonar
49 Firing control
50 Officers' quarters
51 Navigation room
52 Battery circuit breaker
53 'Kuba' and M1H sonar equipment
54 Officers' mess and accommodation for

research personnel
55 Diving tank 4 (port)
56 Diving tank 4 (starboard)
57 STO room
58 Wash room and WCs
59 Battery circuit breaker
60 Two oxygen cylinders
61 Two oxygen cylinders
62 Bow room (forward accommodation
63 Fuel oil bunker 7 (port)
64 Fuel oil bunker 7 (starboard)
65 Freezer (port)
66 Freezer (starboard)
67 Mechanical log apparatus
68 Port drying locker for waterproof clothing
69 Starboard drying locker for waterproof clothing
70 Torpedo compensating tank 2
71 Torpedo compensating tank 1
72 Diving tank 5

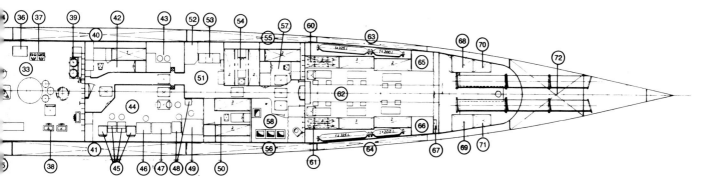

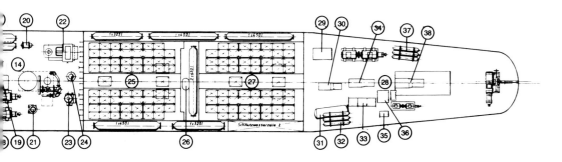

F4   PLAN AT LOWER DECK
     (1/200 scale)

1 Stern compartment
2 Aft hydroplane drive
3 Sewage tank
4 Transformer 1
5 Battery compartment IV 2
6 Air compressor III 2
7 Air compressor III 1
8 Fresh water tank 2
9 Fresh water tank 1
10 Fresh water tank 4
11 Fresh water tank 3
12 Provision store 2
13 Provision store 1
14 Auxiliary machine room
15 Three-way switchboard
16 Radar aerial well
17 Exciter-transformer 2
18 Exciter-transformer 1
19 Schnorkel/periscope well
20 Electric compass transformer
21 Shallow bilge pump
22 Air compressor V
23 Deep bilge pump
24 Electric compass
25 Battery compartment VI 2
26 Cofferdam
27 Battery compartment VI 4

28 Bow torpedo room
29 'Kuba' sonar sector scanner
30 Transformer II (4 kWA)
31 Sewage tank
32 Four oxygen cylinders
33 'Kuba' sonar signal amplifier
34 Transformer I (8 kWA)
35 'Kuba' sonar equipment
36 'Kuba' sonar equipment

NOTES AND ABBREVIATIONS

auxiliary bulkhead (*Hilfsschott*)   a bulkhead necessitated by the sectional construction of the Type XXI (for instance to close off a tank space during construction at the joint between two hull sections – such a bulkhead was usually pierced during assembly of the boat to create the required single tank space).

GHG (*Gruppenhorchgerät*)   the standard array of forty-eight hydrophones in a horizontal ring within the specially-built balcony under the bow of the Type XXI.

KLA (*Kriegsschiffbau-Lehrabteilung*)   the Naval Construction Office.

Kptl (*Kapitänleutnant*)   Lieutenant Commander.

Korvkpt (*Korvettenkapitän*)   Commander.

LUT (*Lagenunabhängiger Torpedo*)   'position independent' or programmable torpedo.

NEK (*Nachrichtenmittel-Erprobungskommando*)   the Communications Trials Command.

NHG (L) (*Nautisches Horchgerät mit Lautsprechern*) hydrophone 'pinger'.

Oblt (*Oberleutnant*)   Lieutenant.

OKM (*Oberkommando der Kriegsmarine*)   the Naval High Command.

Support bulkhead (*Stützschott*)   a bulkhead supporting the outer casing of a U-boat, but not subdividing the pressure hull.

UAK (*Uboot-Abnahme-Kommission*)   the U-boat Acceptance Commission, also used to denote the period during which a U-boat was undergoing acceptance trials.

UZO (*Unterseeboots Ziel Ortungsgerät*)   the surface torpedo-aiming device, which transmitted bearings from the observer on the bridge to the torpedo setters.

PHOTOGRAPH CREDITS